Serving a Higher Purpose

Serving a Higher Purpose

Theosophy for a Meaningful Life

DAVID P. BRUCE

Foreword by
Michael Gomes

QUEST
BOOKS

Theosophical Publishing House
Wheaton, Illinois * Chennai, India

Quest Books
Theosophical Publishing House
P.O. Box 270
Wheaton, IL 60187-0270

www.questbooks.com

Cover image: iStock.com/Jaffar Ali Afzal

Library of Congress Cataloging-in-Publication Data

Names: Bruce, David P., author.
Title: Serving a higher purpose: theosophy for a meaningful life / David P.
  Bruce; foreword by Michael Gomes.
Description: First Quest Edition. | Wheaton, Illinois: Quest Books-Theosophical
Publishing House, 2019. | Includes index.
Identifiers: LCCN 2019000567 | ISBN 9780835609456
Subjects: LCSH: Theosophy.
Classification: LCC BP565.B78 E87 2019 | DDC 299/.934--dc23
LC record available at https://lccn.loc.gov/2019000567

5 4 3 2 * 20 21 22 23

Printed in the United States of America

To my mother, Vera M. Bruce,

who introduced me to Theosophy as a child

and who inspired and encouraged my love of literature

CONTENTS

CHAPTER 11: REFLECTIONS ON *The Voice of the Silence*

CHAPTER 12: REFLECTIONS ON *The Secret Doctrine*

FOREWORD

Anyone who thinks Theosophy is not practical will find this book a revelation. Drawn from introductory letters for courses offered by the Theosophical Society in America, these pieces present clear guidelines for spiritual living in the twenty-first century. These courses from the National Lodge covered a wide array of ethical, religious, and metaphysical themes, and it was David Bruce's lot to provide a one-page lead into the topic at hand. He had to be cogent and concise, to explain but not overwhelm. Written between 2007 and 2018, the letters have retained their relevancy, and the arrangement into helpful categories in this volume makes it even more accessible.

This book is a fount of inspiration by a writer not generally known outside the Theosophical Society. Veteran Theosophist David Bruce, who has held the office of National Secretary of the TS in America for a number of years, puts his insights to use here. He challenges the reader with a number of powerful assertions throughout the book, such as:

- Why should our life bring forth weeds when it can instead be a source of delight and inspiration, not only to us but also to others?

- It is one thing to assert that human existence has a purpose, but quite another to articulate what that purpose is.

- What is the difference between knowledge and wisdom?

Chapters deal with contemporary issues as well as questions to contemplate. Headings such as "Living with Purpose," "Human Nature," and "Spiritual Practice" make the book easy to navigate.

There are also chapters on the Theosophical Society and its Objects, which serve as a helpful guide. There is even a chapter with suggestions on books and thinking that includes reading advice from Annie Besant. The author's wry sense of interpretation can be seen in pieces such as "Why Johnny Can't Meditate" and "Silence—An Endangered Species," which not only identify the problem but also provide prescriptives.

As Bruce indicates, Theosophical literature affirms that there is indeed a purpose underlying human existence. To have any lasting value, the effort we invest in our Theosophical study needs to bear dividends in our daily life. Reflecting on the human condition, he shows that there are no easy shortcuts on the spiritual path. To be in touch with the spiritual side of life, we have to discover our own limits and vulnerabilities to the relentless media barrage, and we can do so only by careful self-observation in which we become aware of how the kaleidoscope of data affects our inner life. He urges the reader to embark on this greatest of all adventures—the treading of the path to Self-Realization.

And it can happen at the least expected times! Bruce describes a "moment of overpowering silence" that occurred when he was stationed in South Korea in 1970. One of his walks took him through a remote rural area: "Across a distant rice paddy, a farmer walked slowly beside an ox that was pulling a wooden cart. They made no sound and appeared not to be in any hurry. . . . It is hard to describe, but the silence had an overpowering quality to it, and it touched me deeply." This experience seems to have abided, for it demonstrates itself throughout the pages of this book.

Bruce recommends that, to live a spiritual life, we need to be capable of experiencing deep inner stillness. To live our life wisely, we need time for quiet and thoughtful reflection. To aid him in this practice, he turns to that wonderful prose poem on spiritual unfoldment, H. P. Blavatsky's *The Voice of the Silence,* to which he devotes two sections of his reflections in this book. Published in 1889, this little guide to the spiritual life has remained in print ever since. Based on *The Book of Golden Precepts*, a text Mme. Blavatsky learned by heart during her training in the East, it charts the steps before the aspirant. The three fragments that she gives outline the yoga stages and the Bodhisattva path before the candidate. The means to advancing on this path can be accessed through six portals or paramitas (virtues). Blavatsky follows the traditional ones given in texts such as Shantideva's *Bodhicaryavatara* and Tsongkhapa's *Lamrim Chenmo.* In her enumeration, she adds one more to make it seven. The paramita *viragaya (*detachment) seems more important today than it may have been a hundred years ago. The ability to remain resilient in the midst of circumstances would certainly be an achievement worth working on.

The seven portals lead forever onward. Initially the way is verdant and inviting, but ahead grey mists "over-hang its rough and stony height." Bruce advocates that careful readers will take time to savor the powerful wordplay found in *The Voice,* thus enhancing their delight and enjoyment of this little masterpiece. To have any lasting value, the effort we invest in our Theosophical study needs to bear dividends in our daily life. At the same time, Bruce adds, statements of Theosophical doctrine are offered not to establish a rigid orthodoxy of verbal formulations but to assist the open-minded inquirer in discovering the reality of eternal and living truths.

The delectable morsels found in the pages of this book serve as a vehicle to discuss and promote Theosophical ideas and at the same time provide an excellent aid in living the spiritual life amid the digital distraction of our interconnected world. Our work, Bruce reminds us, is to plant seeds, the benefits of which we may never see. Reading, concentrated effort, and a desire to understand what we read can be part of our daily *sadhana,* or "spiritual practice." We thereby benefit not only ourselves but, as *Serving a Higher Purpose* points out, our common humanity; for we are deeply connected, not only at the material level but also at the level of thought. Bruce reminds us of St. Paul's advice: "He which soweth sparingly shall reap also sparingly; and he which soweth bountifully shall reap also bountifully" (2 Cor. 9:6). Readers will find a rich harvest in these pages.

—Michael Gomes
New York City

PREFACE

The essays in this book originated between the years of 2007 and 2018 for the National Lodge of the Theosophical Society in America. The National Lodge (NL) is a virtual lodge formed in 1996 for the purpose of providing study courses to members of the Society who do not live near an actual lodge or study center. Although I was living in Wisconsin at the time and was then a member of the Milwaukee Lodge, I also enrolled in the NL in order to benefit from the additional study material.

It was customary for the NL lessons to arrive in the mail accompanied by a one-page cover letter, usually written by the president or the national secretary and consisting of folksy greetings together with news of upcoming events at the national center of the Society in Wheaton, Illinois. They were often embellished with scenic descriptions of the beautiful forty-two-acre campus, especially during the changing of the seasons, and I suppose members who had never visited the national center enjoyed these brief communications.

I joined the staff at TSA headquarters in 2003, being hired by President Betty Bland to serve as director of education. Shortly thereafter, I was given the responsibility of managing the National Lodge. This involved proofreading, formatting, and distributing the study papers. At that time, the members were studying Robert Ellwood's course entitled "Theosophy and World Religions." For the first year or so, I continued the practice of writing one cover letter per lesson. As before, they consisted of salutations from headquarters, an occasional quote from Theosophical literature, and news of current events. They were sincerely written but eminently forgettable.

By the end of 2005, I had tired of producing letters that were too frothy to be of any consequence. Besides, our members could obtain more detailed and timely information on upcoming programs from our burgeoning website. Moreover, I realized that breezy salutations, padded with pastoral sketches of squirrels frolicking on the campus grounds, did very little to promote the cause of Theosophy. So, I began using the letters as a vehicle to discuss and promote Theosophical ideas. Many of the NL members were new to Theosophy, and I thought the letters could be a way of introducing them to basic concepts. In the beginning, the quality of my letters was rather unpolished; even so, I felt they were an improvement over what had gone before. As I continued to develop my writing style, they gradually began taking the form of short but pithy essays. Judging from the comments I received, many of our members found them to be enjoyable, educational, and provocative.

This little bit of background also explains the brevity of the essays, something that even the casual reader will notice at a glance. Originally they were printed on a single page of TSA letterhead, thus limiting the number of words that could be employed. Using a second or third page to write extended essays was considered, but I found that I rather enjoyed the discipline that the constraints of a single page imposed upon me. It forced me to think carefully about what I wanted to say, and it proved quite challenging to write something cohesive and meaningful within those limits. Economy of expression was the order of the day, and every word, every phrase, every sentence was expendable. It was much easier to write a long article, in which one is free to expand, expatiate, or bloviate at length. The process of eliminating superfluous words and phrases helps get to the heart of a matter; it differentiates between what is truly essential and what is merely window dressing and therefore dispensable.

Moreover, a short essay has the virtue of not taking too long to read. Today, people seem to be more preoccupied than ever before, so it seemed to me that essays of modest length would have a better chance of being read. Despite their shortness, I indulge in the hope that some readers will feel that at least a few of these bagatelles may merit repeated readings.

ACKNOWLEDGMENTS

I would like to thank my wife, Donna Wimberley, for her unflagging encouragement throughout the eleven-year process of writing and assembling these essays. Donna read every one of them, and, without her sharp eye and constructive criticism, the overall quality of this work would have suffered. I'd also like to thank Paula Finnegan, a staff member at the national center, who helped with the proofreading of the initial drafts. And I would be remiss if I did not express my gratitude to Sharron Dorr, my skillful editor, who was a joy to work with and whose expertise was invaluable in getting this book ready for publication, and to Nancy Grace, who worked diligently on its production.

EDITOR'S NOTE

To simplify the method of citations in this book, references to two major works of H. P. Blavatsky are cited parenthetically in the text, as follows:

Quotations from *The Voice of the Silence* (originally published in 1889) are taken from the edition reprinted by the Theosophical Publishing House at Adyar, Chennai, in 1982 and indicated in the text by verse number, as in (vs. xx). When some other edition is used, the citation appears as an endnote.

References to *The Secret Doctrine* (originally published in 1888) are taken from the three-volume set reprinted by the Theosophical Publishing House at Adyar, Chennai, in 1979 and indicated in the text by volume and page number, as in (1:yyy).

Finally, references to the Bible are from the King James version. All other references are provided in the endnotes in accordance with standard procedure.

Chapter 1

LIVING WITH PURPOSE

Planting Seeds

*Whatever seeds each man cultivates will grow
to maturity and bear in him their own fruit.*

—PICO DELLA MIRANDOLA,
ORATION ON THE DIGNITY OF MAN

Spring is a time of renewal and new beginnings. After a long midwestern winter, homeowners in the town of Wheaton, Illinois, are busily clearing last fall's debris from their yards. Some are planting spring flowers, thereby bringing a welcome splash of color to the dreary landscape. Others have already started the planting of cool-weather crops in their vegetable gardens.

Our life is like a garden. Our every thought, word, and deed are the "seeds" that sooner or later bear karmic fruit. Whether we eventually harvest flowers or weeds depends on the quality of our actions. Actions harmful toward others inevitably reappear in our garden of life as weeds.

Great spiritual teachers have taught that we reap what we sow. When we truly understand this basic truth, we begin to take responsibility for our thoughts and actions. Why should our life bring forth weeds when it can instead be a source of delight and inspiration, not only to us, but also to others? As the *Voice of the Silence* reminds us, "Sow kindly acts and thou shalt reap their fruition" (vs. 135).

Driving through the community of Wheaton where the national center of the Theosophical Society in America is located, one sees a variety of flower gardens, some small and unimaginative, others large and expansive. When we sow our seeds in the garden of life, how generous are we? Do we settle for a meager display, or do we aim for a pageantry of rich colors and breathtaking beauty?

The words of St. Paul are worth noting: "He which soweth sparingly shall reap also sparingly; and he which soweth bountifully shall reap also bountifully" (2 Cor. 9:6).

Our Divine Potential

It is one thing to assert that human existence has a purpose, but quite another to articulate what that purpose is. Some have said it is to find happiness; others, to live a good life; still others, to glorify God. Beyond the assumption that some divine purpose underlies human existence, there is no consensus as to what that might be. Religious sects are at odds over the best way of honoring and praising the Lord; hedonists and philosophers hold radically different views as to what constitutes the good life; those who are motivated by ideals of service and altruism have a far different understanding of "the pursuit of happiness" than those driven by the need for self-gratification and comfort.

Theosophy answers the question of purpose in broad terms: *We are here to discover and realize our divine potential.* It goes without saying that this is a monumental undertaking, the work not of a day or of a lifetime but of many lifetimes. Throughout this epic journey, the soul garners a wide array of experience, gradually contributing to its spiritual unfoldment on the long path to Self-Realization. And this entire process, which includes hundreds of human incarnations, is governed and regulated by the unwavering law of Karma. As we sow, so shall we reap.

But what can we really know of our ultimate destiny? What can we really know of our unrealized divine potential? If we observe the mass of humanity—both now and throughout history—it appears to be driven not by altruism but by self-interest; not by compassion but ordinary passions; not by distant ideals but by what are perceived to be the needs of the present moment. Yet, if we look closer and observe individuals in action, we may catch glimpses here and there of selfless action—the soldier and firefighter risking their lives as they perform their duties; the teacher and mother tirelessly devoting themselves to the education of the young; the doctor and attorney forgoing a practice based on wealthy clients and instead helping the poor and underprivileged. Examples like this abound if one takes the time to look. These are not saints but ordinary people who have found great meaning and purpose in living for something bigger than the personal self, in discovering that the greatest joy in life is not to take for oneself but to give to others. This is summed up in *The Voice of the Silence* with beautiful simplicity: "To live to benefit mankind" (vs. 144).

A Sure Sense of Purpose

In one of the short stories of Anton Chekhov, a Professor Nikolai Stepanovich approaches his twilight years after enjoying a long, distinguished academic career.[1] During his prime, he was on the faculty of four universities, met all the important people at the upper echelon of society, and was famous throughout Russia. But now he feels a profound sense of emptiness. The triumphs of yesterday ring hollow; fame and recognition have lost their glow. Worse yet, his vast learning has failed to reveal a greater purpose to his life. What was it all for? What did it mean? Stepanovich feels dejected, deflated, depressed.

One suspects that there are many people who feel like this to-day. They've been ambitious; they've worked hard and received awards and accolades, yet they are no longer buoyed by memories of past achievements. There's an uneasy sense that something is missing, something of vital importance. Worldly prizes have lost their luster; self-satisfaction has given way to self-doubt; fulfill-ment to emptiness. What is missing? What have they overlooked?

Fortunate is the man or woman with a sure sense of purpose in life, of being a part of something bigger and grander than the personal self. A few discover it early, others later in life. Some unfortunate souls wander aimlessly without ever finding it. With a sense of purpose, your life is immeasurably enriched. Though you may sense it but dimly, you have an inner conviction that your life is not lived in vain. With or without the spotlights of public recognition, in success or in failure, there is meaning and purpose to your existence. In hard times, you are able to deal with adversity. Difficulties are seen as opportunities to learn valuable life lessons. Confronted by pain and suffering, you somehow find the stamina to prevail. If you have gifts to share with the world, you share them not for personal glory or self-gratification but because you cannot do otherwise.

Without a sense of purpose, life is a charade, shallow and petty. One ends up like Chekhov's professor—sad, lonely, and disillusioned. But now as ever before, the path to discovering your lodestar lies within. Only you can uncover the mystery of your existence.

Yes, but Why?

Over three hundred years ago, René Descartes formulated this simple proposition: "*Cogito, ergo sum*" (I think, therefore I am). To which a modern French philosopher might respond with this riposte: *"Oui, mais pourquoi?"* (Yes, but why?). Nobody in their right mind doubts his or her own existence; but the question as to whether there is a "why" behind the ongoing drama of life continues to engage those with minds given to philosophical reflection.

Theosophical literature affirms that there is indeed a purpose underlying human existence. Our immortal Self repeatedly incarnates in human form for the purpose of realizing its latent divine potential. This process is described as taking place over vast stretches of time and involving cyclical periods of growth known as Root Races, of which there are said to be seven. All this is described in great detail in *The Divine Plan*, Barborka's illuminating commentary on *The Secret Doctrine*. But in the same way that it is easier, from a distance, to see the contour of a forest than of a single tree, the theosophical student may grasp the purpose behind humanity's epic journey more easily than that of his or her own.

It is said that before a soul commences a new incarnation, it sees in a flash a preview of the upcoming life—its purpose, the challenges, the opportunities. That memory resides somewhere in our higher consciousness; in our more intuitive moments, we may catch a rare glimpse of it. But there are more obvious clues that can point us in the right direction. For those with a strong inclination or aptitude for a particular line of work, the advice of the late Joseph Campbell was to "follow your bliss." And our parents may provide a clue. Mozart's father was a professional musician; had he been a banker or businessman, would Mozart's musical genius have flourished in the way that it did? Our circumstances in life also may be trying to tell us something; what we consider to be an obstacle or hardship may be, in fact, an opportunity to develop a certain quality of character that we are lacking. Other clues may be provided by apparent chance occurrences, which are sometimes meaningful synchronicities, intended to guide us in a certain direction.

Whatever our lot in life may be, we would do well to recall an ancient Roman proverb: *Faber est quisque fortunae suae* (Each person is the architect of his own fortune).

Our Most Valuable Possession

If you were to ask me what is the most valuable possession a human being could have, I would say, without hesitation, that it is a deep sense of purpose. With it, a man or woman can bear the greatest of hardships; without it, minor irritants become intolerable. With it, our life acquires richness and depth; without it, our days become increasingly superficial.

If Theosophy tells us anything, it is that there is an underlying purpose to human existence. Yes, there are those who doubt that there is any inherent meaning to life, and some of them are quite well educated, even brilliant. Then there are those who *want* to believe that their life has a purpose, but they aren't satisfied with the simple assurance given from the pulpit that "God has a plan for you." Without having some idea of *what* God's plan is or *how* it may unfold, such declarations seem weak and ineffectual. While most people can rise to meet an occasional crisis, dealing with the drudgery and ennui of an unexciting daily routine can be difficult. God may have a plan for me, but how does sweeping floors, flipping hamburgers, or stocking warehouse shelves fit into that plan?

Today, as in times past, there are those for whom the purpose of life may be summed up as getting an education, pursuing a career, raising a family, and achieving some measure of financial security. No doubt these are laudable goals, but their attainment provides only limited satisfaction. There is a part of our soul that craves something more substantial than worldly success. The words of the Roman poet Persius still bear repeating:

> Young men and old, seek here a purpose for the soul,
> And comfort for the woes that over gray hairs roll.[2]

Although we live in an age dominated by science and technology, it is foolish to go to science for answers to questions that are properly in the domain of philosophy. When the faucet is leaking, you don't call an electrician. Yet many people accept the notion that life has no inherent purpose simply because the scientific establishment has not been able to adduce it through microscopes or test tubes. In this area of human inquiry, the finely honed intuition of a poet or philosopher would be a much better guide than the cold analysis of empiricists. The poet Alfred Lord Tennyson sensed this in the nineteenth century, when he wrote in "Locksley Hall":

> Yet I doubt not thro' the ages one increasing purpose runs,
> And the thoughts of men are widen'd with the process of the suns.

Mme. Blavatsky elaborated on this theme in *The Secret Doctrine*. In the preface, she explains that the rationale for writing the book was "to show that Nature is not 'a fortuitous concurrence of atoms,' and to assign to man his rightful place in the scheme of the Universe" (1: viii). Although contemporary science is not as materialistic as it was in Blavatsky's day, there are still those apostles of materialism who seek to persuade the public that life is nothing but atoms and molecules. This is one reason why there remains a vital need for the message of Theosophy.

Serving a Higher Purpose

Let us acknowledge then that each one has just so much of happiness as he has of virtue and wisdom, and virtuous and wise action.

—Aristotle, *Politics*, Book 7

As discussed in chapter 9 of this book, the second Object of the Theosophical Society encourages members to engage in the "comparative study of religion, philosophy, and science." The third Object asks us to explore nature's "unexplained laws" and the untapped powers that lie dormant within us. A serious and sustained inquiry into either of these Objects could easily involve many years of study, if not lifetimes. But to what end?

In her letter to the 1890 American Convention, H. P. Blavatsky reminds us that our study of Theosophy should ultimately serve a higher purpose than gratifying our momentary curiosity on some metaphysical point or providing us with a veneer of self-importance when discoursing with others on arcane subjects:

> The Ethics of Theosophy are more important than any divulgement of psychic laws and facts. The latter relate wholly to the material and evanescent part of the septenary man, but the Ethics sink in and take hold of the real man—the reincarnating Ego. We are outwardly creatures of but a day; within we are eternal. Learn, then, well the doctrines of Karma and Reincarnation, and teach, practice, promulgate that system of life and thought which alone can save the coming races.[3]

To have any lasting value, the effort we invest in our Theosophical study needs to bear dividends in our daily life. The serious student would do well to ask, "How have my studies made me a more peaceful and loving person? To what extent have I become a force for good in the world?"

It's Never Too Late

Every January, I notice an influx of new people at the local health club. Presumably they are following through on their New Year's resolutions.

As we get older, there's a natural tendency to settle into comfortable grooves and avoid the effort of making new resolutions or exploring new territory. We tell ourselves that we are too old to begin learning Shakespeare, too old to begin appreciating the music of Mozart or Brahms, too old to start reading *The Secret Doctrine*, or too old to begin the practice of meditation.

If a person accepts the notion that we live only one life on this earth followed by an eternity in heaven or some celestial sphere, such attitudes may be understandable. Why make the effort to expand your horizons when the vigor of youth is long gone? What is the point of striving if you have only a few years left? What difference will it make, anyway?

Such attitudes, though prevalent, are shortsighted and based on ignorance. Many years ago, a popular theosophical speaker and writer, Clara Codd, spoke to this issue:

> We must go on from where we are. Some will think they are too old [because] life has almost gone for them. What a mistaken idea! In the life of the Spirit there is no age, nor space nor time as we understand them. . . . A last year of a life, even the last few months, can give a direction, begin a road that continues beyond the confines of death and leads into the next incarnation.[4]

The knowledge that our immortal Self takes incarnation again and again can give us an entirely different perspective on life. As *The Voice of the Silence* says, "Each failure is success, and each sincere attempt wins its rewards in time" (vs. 274).

So, regardless of where you are in life, why not welcome new challenges? Begin your exploration of *The Secret Doctrine*; start your daily meditation practice in earnest; go to your local college and enroll in that philosophy or mathematics course you've always wanted to take. Life is a continuum. The body ages, but the Spirit is timeless.

I'll see you at the health club.

Chapter 2

HUMAN NATURE

Effort Is Required

In some popularized forms of spirituality, words such as *transformation* and *enlightenment* are bandied about so often that you get the impression these are commonplace goods that one can acquire with minimal effort. Opposing this view of easy attainment are those who subscribe to the widespread belief that human nature is what it is—and it can't be changed. One of the Adepts describes human nature as "prejudice based upon selfishness [and] a general unwillingness to give up an established order of things for new modes of life and thought."[1]

Is there a shortage of evidence to support such a dim view of human nature? If you look around at our consumer-oriented society, for example, you may be inclined to agree with the following assessment of human greed and superficiality:

Look at the number of things we buy because others have bought them or because they're in most people's houses. One of the causes of the troubles that beset us is the way our lives are guided by the example of others; instead of being set to rights by reason, we're seduced by convention. There are things that we shouldn't wish to imitate if they were done by only a few, but when a lot of people have started doing them we follow along, as though a practice became more respectable by becoming more common.[2]

Sound familiar? What is striking is that these words come not from an astute observer of contemporary society but from the pen of the Stoic philosopher Seneca, a famous Roman philosopher who lived two thousand years ago. Apparently *some* things haven't changed.

So, the questions remain: Can human nature be changed in a fundamental way? Or are we doomed forever to see the world through the prism of our self-centered ways? To these questions, Theosophy offers an optimistic but realistic response. In *The Secret Doctrine*, H. P. Blavatsky speaks of an "obligatory pilgrimage" that "admits no privileges or special gifts" and that requires "personal effort and merit" over an extended period of human incarnations. In other words, we are all embarked on that "obligatory pilgrimage," whether we realize it or not, but the eventuality of self-transformation will continue to elude those who are unwilling to make the necessary effort. We know this because, first, nothing worthwhile in life is achieved without strenuous effort. And second, we are told by those who have actually achieved these goals that a sustained and monumental effort is required for success. This is a profoundly inspiring and positive message, but one that is also tempered by a realistic view of the undeniable difficulties involved.

The fruits of the spiritual life are there for the taking, but they cannot be reduced to bland commodities sold on the cheap.

Human Nature and Character Development

"Whoever wishes to understand fully the words of Christ must try to pattern his whole life on that of Christ."[3] These words from *The Imitation of Christ* by Thomas á Kempis, a fifteenth-century monk, echo an approach to Christianity that seems to have fallen out of favor in recent times. By contrast, contemporary Christianity places its primary emphasis on salvation by faith in Jesus rather than by doing the hard work of transforming one's character. In

Timothy Keller's *New York Times* bestseller, *The Reason for God*, the author flatly states that it's a mistake to view the Christian faith as "a form of moral improvement."[4]

Some people say you can't change human nature, or at least that you can only in a marginal sense. It's not hard to compile evidence in support of this argument. On the other hand, many of us have witnessed friends or family members who have made great strides in character, often as a result of struggling valiantly with some personal problem or challenge that they were forced to face. Speaking as a Theosophist, the belief that you can't change human nature strikes me as nothing more than a convenient excuse to avoid doing the hard work required for living a life reflective of the teachings found in, say, the Sermon on the Mount or the guidelines found in H. P. Blavatsky's "The Golden Stairs" (see appendix A).

What is the best way to go about changing ourselves? Aristotle once noted that "excellence of character results from habit,"[5] meaning that there must be a consistency of effort put forth over a period of time. In this regard, Benjamin Franklin devised a practical approach of working on only one virtue for each month of the year. The trials and tribulations of daily life provide the battleground where our good resolve is tested. Good character cannot be wished into existence; it takes a sustained effort and must be developed in the hustle and bustle of daily existence. As the German poet Goethe observed, "Talents are nurtur'd best in solitude, a character on life's tempestuous sea."[6]

Some Things Don't Change

Has human nature changed over the past thousands of years? Those who lack a sense of history may not know the answer to that question. In an age when everything seems to be changing at a rapid pace, they ask, why not human nature?

The technological marvels achieved by science over the past hundred years are truly astounding. The science fiction writer Arthur C. Clarke once said, "Any sufficiently advanced technology is indistinguishable from magic."[7] Today, the prevailing attitude in some quarters is that, given enough time, there is no problem science cannot solve. With regard to the material world, this may be so, but what about basic human nature? Are the universally recognized flaws of human nature amenable to technological solutions? Only the most naïve would think so.

Reflecting upon the human condition, H. P. Blavatsky said, "Civilization may progress, [but] human nature will remain the same throughout all ages."[8] Despite the "magic" of modern science, the age-old vices such as avarice, laziness, and vanity continue to flourish. In some cases, technology even facilitates bad behavior, as demonstrated by the proliferation of salacious videos found on YouTube, the obsessive texting on cell phones while driving, and the sometimes uncivil and vulgar Web postings by legions of anonymous bloggers. Speaking of bad behavior, the following observation seems to describe the cult of celebrity that is so typical of our times:

> The person who lives extravagantly wants their manner of living to be on everybody's lips as long as they are alive. They think they are wasting their time if they are not being talked about. So every now and then they do something calculated to set people talking. Plenty of people squander fortunes, plenty of people keep mistresses. To win any reputation in this sort of company you need to go in for something not just extravagant but really out of the ordinary. In a society as hectic as this one it takes more than common profligacy to get oneself talked about.[9]

If you wonder whether human nature has changed over time, you may want to consult history. The above quote comes from the writings of Seneca, a Roman philosopher who lived two millennia ago.

Some Things Can Change

It takes years of post-graduate study to become an attorney; it takes years of grueling physical workouts to become a professional athlete; it takes years of intense practice and training to become a concert pianist—assuming one has the requisite raw talent and mental or physical aptitude to begin with.

I grant you that none of this is exactly a news flash. Yet for some inexplicable reason, people hearing about self-transformation for the first time often think they can achieve it by going to a few workshops or by listening to motivational CDs in their spare time.

The spiritual neophyte would be well advised to study history and face this one enduring fact: human nature is full of flaws, frailties, and shortcomings. To delude one's self into thinking otherwise is to court failure and even abandonment of the quest. Christians have long recognized this. As a young man about town, St. Augustine struggled with the passions of his lower nature because he "knew not how to conceive of anything beyond corporeal splendors."[10] When he decided to follow Christ, he still had to do battle with his in-grained habits of sensuality and physical gratification.

In one of his letters to A. P. Sinnett, the Master K. H. said, "As for human nature in general, it is the same now as it was a million . . . years ago."[11] Are we really surprised by that statement? We shouldn't be. If transformation were that easy, there would be more Adepts with glowing auras than there are shoppers at Walmart the day after Thanksgiving.

The message that we can take from studying the lives of deeply spiritual people is that self-transformation is possible, but it is not the work of a few short months or years. From the theosophical point of view, it may require not only years, but lifetimes. Speaking from experience, the Master K. H. described it this way: "The adept is the rare efflorescence of a generation of enquirers."[12] Translation: there are no easy shortcuts on the spiritual path.

All this is said not to discourage anybody but rather to provide a realistic expectation as to the difficulties and hardships involved. To embark on this greatest of all adventures—the treading of the path to Self-Realization—brings not only tears but sublime joy beyond our imagining. To reach those lofty heights, however, the aspiring pilgrim needs the mental discipline of an attorney, the stamina of an athlete, and the sensitivity of a concert pianist.

The Illusion of Separateness

In the 1948 film *Red River*, considered by many critics to be one of the best Westerns ever made, John Wayne gives a memorable performance as Tom Dunson, an unyielding and stubborn man driven by ruthless ambition. Early in the film, there is an iconic scene where Dunson, in the midst of a vast and desolate prairie, abruptly decides to break away from the group of settlers bound for California and head south into Texas to seek his fortune in the cattle business. Dunson embodies the archetype of a lone and solitary figure, ready to square off against the world with an air of self-assured defiance in pursuit of personal glory.

With all due respect to the time-honored qualities of self-reliance and self-initiative—virtues commonly associated with this archetype—no one really lives a completely independent life, alone and apart from the rest of humanity. To think otherwise is to indulge in whimsy. Each of us is interconnected in so many ways, and at so many levels, that we tend to overlook this obvious fact: our existence depends on the existence of countless others, the vast majority of whom we will never ever meet.

Consider those western-style jeans you're wearing, which you probably take for granted. How many hands played a part in their creation? Who provided the denim? Who made the dye? Who constructed the zipper? Who made the design? How many hands were needed to gather the raw materials and deliver them to the manufacturer in time for production? And, after all that, someone had to sew those jeans. Someone had to deliver them to the retailer. Someone had to create ads to draw customers. On and on it goes, an endless web of connections, all of which are necessary to produce a single piece of apparel.

We *are* connected with the rest of humanity—and in more ways than we might imagine. This is a fundamental principle of Theosophy, one that manifests in even the most mundane and ordinary aspects of our daily existence.

The Pervasive Appeal of Superficiality

It should not come as a revelation to any thinking person that certain aspects of our popular culture engender a superficial state of mind. A steady diet of the daily news can lead to a state of agitation; being plugged into various social media without pause can result in a distracted mind; and the quickness of electronic media may delude us into thinking that the process of self-discovery requires no more effort than performing a routine search on Google.

To discover the inner Self is the work of a lifetime. The disciplines practiced by generations of yogis and seers are aimed at developing a mind that is steady, one-pointed, and able to pierce the veils of illusion, or *māyā*. This requires one to stand apart from the crowd and not mistake the passing illusions of life for reality. James Fenimore Cooper wrote that "All greatness of character is dependent on individuality. The man who has no other existence than that which he partakes in common with all around him, will never have any other than an existence of mediocrity."[13] William Ralph Inge, a professor of divinity at Cambridge and Dean of St. Paul's Cathedral, put it more succinctly: "He who marries the spirit of the age will soon be a widower."

This is not to suggest that we adopt an attitude of denying the world or escapism; we all have our parts to play in the drama of life. But those with discernment recognize that there exists a greater reality beyond the surface appearances that enthrall the senses. The spirit will endure after the persona perishes. Meanwhile, there is a balance we must maintain between the inner and the outer, the surface and the depths, if we are to lead a spiritual life while living in a busy and ever-changing world. Where that point of balance is found will be determined by each individual. But, sadly, some are oblivious to anything but the surface of life. As theologian Paul Tillich noted in his essay "The Depth of Existence,"

> It is comfortable to live on the surface so long as it remains un-shaken. It is painful to break away from it and descend into an unknown ground. The tremendous amount of resistance against that act in every human being and the many pretexts invented to avoid the road to the depth are natural. The pain of looking into one's own depth is too intense for most people. . . . But eternal joy is not to be reached by living on the surface. It is rather attained by breaking through the surface, by penetrating the deep things of ourselves, of our world, and of God.[14]

But such a condition of superficiality is not permanent. According to Theosophy, each soul will learn eventually to penetrate the surface and probe the depths of life in its fullness.

The Secular Trinity, Part 1

For those souls driven relentlessly by worldly ambition, the secular trinity of wealth, fame, and power prevails. Yet even among those possessing more modest levels of ambition, who has not at one time or another longed for more money, wider recognition, or a larger sphere of influence? Who has not felt—if only briefly—the desire to propitiate and kneel before these secular gods? Some think that being rich would solve all their problems, that being powerful would make life exciting, that being famous would make them happy. But as the Buddha and other spiritual teachers have observed, these worldly prizes are essentially nothing more than ephemera.

Those of us attempting to lead a spiritual life might reflect as to whether our hearts are still capable of being stirred, ever so faintly, by these secular gods. Have we really understood their illusory nature? Have we really become immune to their siren call? Or has our rejection of them been merely a *pro forma* declaration, based perhaps on the fact that we lack the ambition, the assiduity, or the wherewithal to attain them in the first place?

It is fairly easy for some to eschew money and power, but what about recognition and reputation? According to the Roman historian Tacitus, "Even with philosophers the passion for fame is the last weakness to be discarded."[15] Fame can outlast us, while wealth and power are dissipated upon our demise, if not before. Worldly power is subject to the winds of fortune; money and possessions can be lost in a flash; but if one writes a book one may be remembered a hundred years from now, thus gaining a little whiff of immortality.

In spite of our vigilance to be selfless, the yearning for recognition can subsist as a subtle and persistent psychological force. One effective method of dealing with it is to seek opportunities for helping others without any thought of personal gain. The paradox is that by focusing on the needs of another, we become more alive and vibrant without thinking about ourselves. This advice is succinctly given in *The Voice of the Silence:* "Give up thy life, if thou would'st live" (vs. 21).

The Secular Trinity, Part 2

In the last essay, I made this observation: "For those souls driven relentlessly by worldly ambition, the secular trinity of wealth, fame, and power prevails." Let us now consider power and its relation to the spiritual life.

It is a commonplace that power corrupts. Although that may not always be the case, history offers numerous examples to support that view. The Irish statesman Edmund Burke noted, "The greater the power, the more dangerous the abuse."[16] Certainly, the *potential* for harm and mischief parallels the degree to which power is vested in a person. Some have taken an even more cynical view. "Power is not a means, it is an end," says novelist George Orwell.[17] In his *Leviathan*, English philosopher Thomas Hobbes states, "I put for a general inclination of all mankind, a perpetual and restless desire of power after power that ceaseth only in death."[18] History affords many instances of the corrosive effect of power on the moral fiber of those who wield it, not only in the secular realm, but in the religious realm as well.

In view of such warnings, what is the role of power in the spiritual life? Is it something to be shunned or feared? "Except ye be converted, and become as little children, ye shall not enter into the kingdom of heaven" (Matt. 18:3). Or is the possession of power compatible with living a Theosophical or spiritual life? Mabel Collins would answer in the affirmative: "Desire power ardently."[19]

By definition, power is what enables a person to act, to produce an effect, or to achieve a desired end. As such, power per se is neither good nor bad. Such judgments relate only to how that power is used, i.e., whether it is used selfishly or altruistically. Jesus and Buddha had great power—the power to influence millions of lives for the better. Joseph Stalin had great power, which he abused in his ruthless quest for political domination, thereby causing untold suffering and millions of deaths. George Orwell was right: for despots such as Stalin, power is an end in itself. But for the great spiritual teachers of humanity, Orwell's view does not apply. For them, power is a means, not an end.

There is one other crucial difference, articulated by Huston Smith: "Unlike spiritual values, wealth, fame, and power do not multiply when shared. They cannot be given away without reducing your own portion."[20]

The Secular Trinity, Part 3

What is the true measure of wealth? In all ages there are those who dedicate their lives to its pursuit. But what is wealth? It may, and often does, translate to money; but there are other ways to gauge wealth. In fact, finding a universal definition of it proves somewhat elusive. Why is that? The answer is that "wealth" is a moving target. By this, I mean that the concept of wealth is both *relative* and *subjective*, depending on the circumstances. A person in the United States who is living under the official poverty line and yet has a cell phone, a flat-screen TV, air conditioning, and an SUV may be considered wealthy relative to the millions of people eking out a subsistent standard of living in some parts of the world. A millionaire may feel impoverished when contemplating the lifestyle of a billionaire.

The idea of wealth is also subjective. For the Wall Street banker, it may consist of a large and balanced portfolio of stocks, bonds, and liquid assets. For the scholar who has spent her whole life in books, it may consist of an immense and detailed knowledge regarding her chosen field of study. For the social worker, it may be measured by the many lives that he has helped throughout his career. And for the grandmother, it may consist of a lifetime of warm and loving memories, which are the dividends of raising a large family.

John Ruskin once said, "There is no wealth but life."[21] By that, I think he was referring to the miracle of being alive: to play one's role on the stage of life; to respond to the beauty of life, as well as its tragedies; to share laughter with friends, tears with loved ones; to give freely of oneself; to discover the fulfillment that comes from achieving a worthwhile dream; and to know that one has lived a good life.

But to the altruistic soul, the true measure of wealth is in the giving. Clara Codd was such a person, devoting her life to Theosophical work around the world. In her autobiography, she closes with these inspiring words: "A new age, a new world is being hammered out on the anvil of time, an age in which both war and poverty will cease to be. Do not let us desire in these tremendous times personal comfort and easy living. Let us be willing to forgo much, that the future for which so many of our best youth died may be secure."22

The Secular Trinity, Part 4

Human beings are complex creatures, often motivated by conflicting aims and desires. We vacillate between modesty and pretentiousness, frugality and self-indulgence, ethicality and expediency, and many other such polar opposites. The spiritual pilgrim experiences this same inner conflict, at least in the earlier stages on the path. An interior impulse is felt, and the decision is made to dedicate oneself to a certain way of living. Then that pilgrim is sooner or later tested by various distractions, thus revealing his resoluteness or lack thereof.

The spiritual impulse in younger souls, however genuine it may be, is easily overpowered by the loud clamor for worldly success. The prizes offered by the world generally fall into three categories: wealth, power, and fame. Although these can be powerful motivators for overachievers, they are, from the standpoint of spirit, largely illusory. Wealth and power can be lost overnight; and, unlike the fruits of a sanctified life, they cannot be taken across the threshold of death. There are those who, realizing the temporary nature of wealth and power, seek out fame and celebrity as a proxy for immortality. As the historian Tacitus once noted, the last worldly goal to be relinquished is the thirst for fame and glory.[23]

Some may think it possible to achieve great renown and live a life of inner purity. Experience has shown this not to be possible or even practical. Fame may come to a spiritual person, but if it arrives it is incidental. It is as true today as it was in days of old: one simply cannot serve two masters. Plutarch, a historian from antiquity who understood human nature, made this insightful observation: "The desire of glory has great power in washing the tinctures of philosophy out of the souls of men."[24]

If one should manage to achieve popular acclaim and luminary status, there is a price to pay. First, one must feverishly work to keep it from slipping away. Then there is the loss of privacy and the fact that it becomes difficult to distinguish true friends from celebrity seekers. As Montaigne stated, "Fame and tranquility can never be bedfellows."[25] The fleeting nature of fame is expressed by this Roman maxim: *Sic transit gloria mundi* (The glories of the world are fleeting).

Yours may be a household name today, but it will likely draw blank stares from future generations. You may have a street named after you today, but names can be changed. That hard-sought fame that you dedicated your life to achieving will, in the end, fade from view faster than the blue dye in a pair of cheap denim jeans.

The Spark of Enthusiasm

People who are drawn to the teachings of Theosophy are attracted to them in varying degrees. If one were to construct a composite graph measuring the intensity of each person's attraction to the wisdom teachings, it would form a type of continuum. Furthermore, that continuum would appear to be divided into three stages. Let us label these stages in terms of relative intensity, from weakest to most potent: *curiosity*, *interest*, and *enthusiasm*.

By its very nature, curiosity is often short lived, being easily satisfied with superficialities and pleasantries; this fact results in its moving on in search of further attractions (or distractions). Information on chakras, auras, telepathy, past-life memories, out-of-body experiences, and psychic abilities typically draws the attention of those who are driven primarily by curiosity.

But curiosity can lead to a deeper exploration of the wisdom teachings, one that is characterized by a persistent level of inquiry. At this stage, curiosity has been replaced by a level of sustained interest. The casual inquirer has now become a student, seeking out detailed knowledge by reading theosophical literature, listening to lectures, attending discussion groups, participating in workshops—and doing so on a regular basis. Whereas the initial attraction was intermittent and superficial, that curiosity has deepened into a serious interest characterized by consistency and regularity in the pursuit of knowledge.

But one's interest in a subject may fade or diminish in time; or one may be content to stay within a certain prescribed area instead of expanding into related areas of knowledge. On the other hand, it may be transformed into a deeper level of inquiry if the necessary catalyst or conditions are present. For example, if the teachings begin to resonate deeply and not just serve as an amusing intellectual pastime; or if a dynamic speaker motivates and inspires the listener to a new level, based on the speaker's level of conviction; or if an author articulates a difficult or mystifying aspect of the teachings in a clear and convincing manner, then something very important and essential may occur—the spark of *enthusiasm* may ignite. When this happens, the quest for knowledge begins to burn with a brightness and intensity that was previously lacking. With genuine enthusiasm, theosophical study becomes not merely an interesting pursuit but a lifetime preoccupation, essential to the soul's sense of purpose and well-being. And that is why a former TSA president, L. W. Rogers, once said, "Enthusiasm is a thing of priceless value."[26]

Chapter 3

ON BOOKS AND THINKING

Why Read?

When we do something again and again, the force of habit takes over and we often lose sight of why we are doing it in the first place. Take reading, for example. Many people spend countless hours reading, whether books or magazines or online. They probably don't ever pause to ask why they read; they just do it. To ask why a person reads is like asking why one breathes. Who would ask such a question? Only a simpleton would, or maybe a philosopher.

Four hundred years ago, the philosopher Francis Bacon asked that very same question. Since Theosophists love to read, it may be useful for us to consider Bacon's analysis. In a short, but pithy, essay entitled "Of Studies," Bacon gave three reasons for reading: *delight*, *ornament*, and *ability*.[1] Let's take each one in turn. Theosophical study offers the sublime delight and satisfaction that comes from gaining a deeper understanding of life and the world we live in. By ornamentation, Bacon meant the ability to converse about what we have read. Anyone who has been to a Theosophical convention has surely witnessed this, for Theosophists love to talk about the books they have read. The third reason—ability—is the capacity to apply what one has learned. Bacon also noted that there can be drawbacks to each of these three motivations: reading only for enjoyment leads to laziness; reading only to acquire knowledge leads to ostentation; reading only to decide how to make decisions leads to an academic literal-mindedness. As in so many things in life, it comes down to a matter of balance and moderation.

But of the three—delight, ornament, and ability—the third is most relevant to Theosophists, because it facilitates the process of self-transformation. If my reading is not making me a better person, then better not to read and find some other means of self-improvement. As the Roman statesman Cicero said in his oration *Pro Archia*, "Character without learning has made for excellence and ability more often than learning without character."[2] Or, as H. P. Blavatsky said so poetically in *The Voice of the Silence*, "Even ignorance is better than head-learning with no Soul-Wisdom to illuminate and guide it" (vs. 113).

An instance of "character without learning" was given by the British explorer Wilfred Thesiger in his book *Arabian Sands*. Thesiger was the first European to cross the Empty Quarter of the southern Arabian Peninsula on foot, a dangerous and desolate region that contains the largest sand desert in the world. Although he was well educated, Thesiger had this to say about the nomadic desert people whom he came to respect and love: "I shall always remember how often I was humbled by those illiterate herdsmen who possessed, in so much greater measure than I, generosity and courage, endurance, patience, and lighthearted gallantry. Among no other people have I ever felt the same sense of personal inferiority."[3]

The Guiding Light of History

Many years ago, when I was a youngster in high school, like most of my peers I found the study of history to be somewhat less than exciting. It was a rare teacher who had the ability to make history come alive. But as I grew older, my interest in history blossomed, prompting me to explore a wide variety of books on historical figures and bygone eras. Perhaps an appreciation of history is a function of age.

Americans are not noted for their grasp of history. A study conducted in 2008 by the Intercollegiate Studies Institute found that 70 percent of Americans were unable to pass a basic test on core history and civics; less than one-half of those surveyed could name the three branches of American government. In 2007, after conducting a survey of 14,000 college freshmen, the ISI found that the average test score for civic literacy was an appalling 50.4 percent. Freshmen attending elite Ivy League schools hardly fared much better, averaging an embarrassing 64 percent on the same test. The economist Thomas Sowell once observed, "Everything seems new to those too young to remember the old and too ignorant of history to have heard about it."[4]

This is not the time or place to speculate on the reasons for such dismal statistics, but it's worth noting that both the Theosophical Society and the esoteric ideas associated with the Ageless Wisdom have their own colorful and distinct history. Why is this of any importance, you may ask? Here's why. For the Society to continue to flourish, dedicated members should have a degree of interest in the history of our movement as well as the perennial ideas that constitute modern Theosophy. While memorizing names and dates is of marginal value, it seems that serious members should strive to develop a basic understanding of the reasons for which the Theosophical Society was founded; they should be able to articulate what the founders viewed as its fundamental mission in the world. Consider these words from the nineteenth-century French historian Alexis de Tocqueville: "With the past no longer shedding light on the future, the mind advances in darkness."[5]

Why History Is Alive Today

The study of history is a subject that likely holds scant appeal for the young. Interest in the past is not a high priority at that stage of life, easily eclipsed by the imposing immediacy of the present and the alluring promise of the future. For example, I grew up during the 1950s, and World War II seemed to me something that had happened in the distant past; but I'm sure it was very real to my father, who had served in the army during the war. When you are only eight years old, an event from the previous decade might as well have taken place in the previous century. You can't properly relate to it or understand how it has anything to do with your life, because the perspective that comes with time has not had time to develop. At that age, viewing historical events is like looking through the wrong end of a pair of binoculars, with all the images appearing much farther away than they really are.

In my case, an appreciation for history was something I gained much later. That's probably true for most adults. Yet there are some who never see the significance of history and fail to see how it matters. I am reminded of the cranky old character in one of Flannery O'Connor's short stories, of whom the author says: "He didn't have any use for history because he never expected to meet it again."[6] But in life, as in short stories, the unexpected often happens, and actions from the past frequently have repercussions in the present.

Theosophy refers to the principle of cyclicity as being one of the fundamental truths of existence. Time is seen as unfolding in a cyclical, recurring manner rather than in a straight, linear fashion. Regarding the importance of history, Sri Madhava Ashish puts it this way: "Why worry about what happened up till now? The answer is that what has happened in the past has made us what we are now. And what we think about ourselves now determines our attitude towards the future."[7] A truism often attributed to Mark Twain is that, while history may not repeat, it surely does rhyme.

For the Theosophist, history is alive. In fact, we *are* history. You and I have seen the building of the pyramids along the Nile, the aqueducts of ancient Rome, the great cathedrals of Europe, the shipyards of medieval Venice. We have lived through wars and famine, good times and bad. Our home has been the jungle, the desert, the mountains, and the great plateaus. History is not something apart from us; it has molded us, shaped us, and is very much a part of us.

An Avalanche of Books

So many books, so little time. Such is the lament of the poor bibliophile in a world where hundreds of thousands of books are published each year. In my younger days I felt there was ample time to peruse the great literature of the world; what I didn't have time for then could wait till tomorrow. But with the passing of years comes a growing realization that one's allotted time is a diminishing commodity, that discernment in one's reading habits is needed if one is to become acquainted with the profound thoughts of great minds.

Fifteen centuries before Johannes Gutenberg invented the printing press, the philosopher Seneca offered this practical advice to a friend who enjoyed reading:

> You should be extending your stay among writers whose genius is unquestionable, deriving constant nourishment from them if you wish to gain anything from your reading that will find a lasting place in your mind. To be everywhere is to be nowhere.[8]

That continues to be good advice. To know a little about many things is of far less value than having deep knowledge of a few essentials. In his 1858 essay entitled "Books," Ralph Waldo Emerson warned the reader "not to waste his memory on a crowd of mediocrities."[9] Of the multitude of books published each year, how many will be worth reading twenty-five years from now? If we believe the sales and marketing pitches from the publishers, each author is an unqualified "genius," each new book an instant "classic." Emerson, however, placed great value on books that had withstood the test of Time, "who sits and weighs, and ten years hence out of a million of pages prints one. Again, it is judged, it is winnowed by all the winds of opinion, and what terrific selection has not passed on it, before it can be reprinted after twenty years, and reprinted after a century!"[10]

This year an avalanche of books will be published. In time, a select few of them may end up being considered classics, but most will be forgotten within the span of a few years. So read the latest books, if you wish, and familiarize yourself with what contemporary writers have to say. But why not set aside a portion of your time to become acquainted with those durable works of literature, i.e., the classics, which have already been vetted by previous generations of thoughtful readers and which therefore have the proven capacity to provide nourishment and inspiration for the soul?

Discriminative Wisdom

For the student of Theosophy, one big advantage of living today is the abundance of information available. In the early years of the Theosophical Society, only a few books existed—books such as H. P. Blavatsky's *Isis Unveiled* (1877) and A. P. Sinnett's *The Occult World* (1881) and *Esoteric Buddhism* (1883). But today's inquirer has access to hundreds of books, articles, and recordings on various aspects of Theosophy, many of them appearing online.

On the other hand, one big disadvantage for today's student of Theosophy is precisely the abundance of information available. Too much information can be a double-edged sword by making it easier to focus on quantity instead of quality. There is a tendency in many of us (myself included) to move on too quickly to the next book before we have really understood and absorbed the contents of the one just read. I. K. Taimni understood this:

> Most aspirants—and especially those of a scholarly type—suffer
> from the erroneous idea that they have to acquire more and more
> intellectual knowledge and fill their mind with ideas in order to be
> able to know the truths of the inner life. . . . So they read more and
> more books and go on piling up scraps of information in their mind
> without exercising any kind of discrimination in the matter. . . . The
> result of this misdirected effort to grow fat intellectually as quickly
> as possible is similar to what happens when we try to eat more and
> more food with a view to getting physically stronger without suffi-
> cient exercise to digest and assimilate that food. There is intellectual
> indigestion and our mind becomes clogged and burdened with half-
> digested ideas clouding our perception.[11]

Here we have yet another example of how we can exercise the first
qualification for the path described in books such as Jiddu Krishnamurti's *At the Feet of the Master*: discriminative wisdom (*viveka*).
It is important to read books dealing with the spiritual life, but it
is equally if not more important to spend time reflecting and assimilating what we read. Until we have done that, we cannot make
those ideas a part of our life.

Facts and Principles

Many people find reading *The Secret Doctrine* to be a difficult
undertaking, quickly becoming discouraged and giving up in
frustration. Why is it such a daunting task? There may be many
reasons, but one frequent complaint is that "it's too abstract." The
implication is that the highly theoretical principles described in
The Secret Doctrine have little to do with everyday life. This raises
some interesting philosophical questions: Is an abstraction less
real than something that is tangible? Is an abstraction less relevant
to our lives than something we can see and touch with our own
hands? It seems that for some people, a concrete object is more real

than any abstract principle. So let us consider the relation between a fact and a principle.

Scientific folklore has it that Isaac Newton formulated his theory of gravity after observing an apple fall to the ground. What was of significance was not the fact that an apple had fallen to the ground, but the discovery of the principle of gravity. Would it have made any difference if the falling object had been a ripe orange, or even a coconut? A falling grapefruit or pineapple would have demonstrated the force of gravity just as effectively. Clearly the falling object is not what was important, but rather the scientific law behind the action. What Newton observed was merely the outer and temporary effects of a timeless principle at work—the law of gravity.

The human mind has the capacity to think in both concrete and abstract terms. When we think of a dog, we can think of a particular dog, or we can think of dogs in general. Theosophy refers to the higher and lower mind, but these are terms used to describe two very different functions of a single mind. The observation of empirical data is a function of the lower mind, as when we remember the color, shape, and texture of a piece of clothing. Thought, in terms of concepts and principles such as justice, truth, and beauty, is a function of the higher mind. As human beings, we need and use both faculties.

The multitude of strange terms and stories in *The Secret Doctrine* can easily lead to a state of confusion if the reader loses sight of the fundamental principles involved—unity, polarity, and periodicity. If you find yourself struggling with *The Secret Doctrine*, overwhelmed by obscure terms and esoteric arcana, this is a sign that you have become bogged down in the minutia of details while losing sight of the overarching principles.

Incidentally, there is a direct parallel here to how we live our lives. Without a set of guiding principles, we are like a boat without a rudder out on the open sea. Statements of principles *are* abstract;

but once they are understood, we can rely on them with confidence
to help us navigate the inevitable storms and vicissitudes of life.

The Tangible and the Intangible

No doubt you've heard the popular expression "keeping it real."
As a member of the baby-boomer generation, I confess to reacting
to such colloquialisms with a mixture of amusement and mild an-
noyance. To my way of thinking, the phrase "keeping it real" has
nothing to do with seeking out lasting values in life and everything
to do with adapting one's mode of dress, speech, and behavior to
the trendy and tenuous fashions of the day. Such a perspective
comes with age, and I admit that my generation had its repertoire
of youthful slang, as I'm sure is the case for each generation.

In a recent essay, I raised the question as to whether an abstraction was less real than a tangible object. Let's explore that question
through numbers. Take, for example, the number three, something that any five-year-old can understand. But wait. Have you
ever seen three? Your immediate reaction might be "yes, countless
times." But have you? I submit that what you've seen were merely
illustrations of the number three—three apples, three bottles,
three shirts, or even its numerical symbol—but you've never actually seen three in its pure essence. And you never will. A pure
number is a mathematical abstraction. A bowl of three red apples
provides a tangible example of the number three, but when those
apples are eaten, the concept of three continues unchanged while
the apples are no more. So, which is more real: the number three as
an abstract principle, or three freshly picked red apples?

H. P. Blavatsky said that the Theosophical Society was formed
to show mankind that "such a thing as Theosophy exists, and to
help [us] ascend towards it by studying and assimilating its eternal
verities."[12] You may gain an understanding of the eternal verities,

but you'll never see or touch them in the empirical sense, as they do not belong to this world of finite and ephemeral objects. Truth exists outside time, casting its periodic reflection on the temporal world through the purified thoughts and actions of human beings. When one is talking about "keeping it real," I believe, this is about as real as it gets.

Reading Advice from Annie Besant

In her book *Thought Power: Its Control and Culture*, Annie Besant offers some useful advice for developing the power of the mind.[13] While many people are avid readers, she says merely reading a book from cover to cover does little to develop the mind. Reading the printed words on a page is one thing; thinking about what they mean is another. The process of thinking about what we have just read, she says, is what builds our cognitive powers. If we read quickly through a difficult book, what have we gained? How much of the author's thought have we really understood? Being able to repeat the author's words verbatim is a function of memory, not of understanding. If we truly understand the ideas put forth by an author, we should be able to convey them using our own words.

Besant offers a simple technique that anybody can apply to his or her daily reading session. Simply put, it amounts to reading less and thinking more, by a ratio of 2:1. Let's say that you are going to set aside an hour each day to read a book of substance. Many people assume they are making progress by reading as many pages as possible during a given period of time. Annie Besant likens this to filling the stomach with food, but without digesting it and assimilating its nutrients. Her suggestion is to read for five minutes, then pause and think for ten, and so on throughout the hour. After five minutes of reading, we might ask: What were the author's key points? Do I agree? What didn't I understand? If we follow this pattern, our sixty-minute reading session will include twenty minutes of substantive reading and forty minutes of strenuous thinking. This method may seem arduous at first, especially if a person is not accustomed to prolonged mental effort. But, like anything else, it gets easier with practice. Naturally, we are talking about applying this method to books of substance, not books intended for light reading or mere entertainment.

If we adopt this simple discipline and use it on a regular basis, says Annie Besant, we will notice such benefits as increased powers of concentration, clarity of thought, and depth of understanding.

Recommended Theosophical Reading

A question often asked by those who have recently discovered Theosophy is, "What shall I read?" It's a good question; the newcomer can easily get lost in the bewildering number of books falling under the broad heading of Theosophy. Longtime students will have no problem coming up with their lists of recommended reading, but those lists will vary according to individual preferences. Before compiling such a list, I would keep in mind the advice of Francis Bacon:

> Some books are to be tasted, others to be swallowed, and some few
> to be chewed and digested; that is, some books are to be read only in
> parts; others to be read, but not curiously [with minute attention];
> and some few to be read wholly, and with diligence and attention.[14]

The first category might include reference works, for example, H. P. Blavatsky's *Theosophical Glossary* or Geoffrey Barborka's *Glossary of Sanskrit Terms*. It might also include books containing quotes to be used for meditation, such as *Thoughts for Aspirants* by N. Sri Ram and various compilations or anthologies that have been published throughout the years.

In the second category, I would place *The Key to Theosophy* by Blavatsky; *The Inner Life* and *Masters and the Path,* both by C. W. Leadbeater; historical books such as Michael Gomes's *The Dawning of the Theosophical Movement* and Howard Murphet's biography of H. P. Blavatsky, *When Daylight Comes*; and substantive but easy-to-read books such as *The Astral Body* by A. E. Powell and *At the Feet of the Master* by Krishnamurti.

Finally, the third category should include (no surprise here) *The Secret Doctrine* and *The Voice of the Silence,* both by Blavatsky; *The Mahatma Letters to A. P. Sinnett*; Barborka's *The Divine Plan*; and a few other hearty mainstays of the Theosophical repertoire.

The titles noted above are not meant to provide a comprehensive listing but rather are suggestions illustrative of certain categories. Specific recommendations will vary from Theosophist to Theosophist. What holds true, I think, is Bacon's astute observation that not all books are meant to be read in the same manner. Just as in dining, where it is best not to confuse appetizers with the main course, when it comes to reading, some books serve only to whet the palate, whereas others can provide nourishment for years and years to come.

Chapter 4

SPIRITUAL PRACTICE

The Importance of Meditation

Go placidly amid the noise and the haste,
and remember what peace there may be in silence.

— MAX EHRMANN, "DESIDERATA"

To engage in the regular practice of meditation does not mean that we enclose ourselves in a hermetically sealed cocoon of bliss, remaining oblivious to events in the outer world. In fact, meditation better allows us to cope with the pressures of the outer world, not by providing us a means of escape but by enabling us to face those challenges calmly and insightfully. The experienced meditator draws strength and confidence from a deep reservoir of inner peace and wisdom, which is brought about by many years of meditative practices.

But we can also make the mistake of immersing ourselves too much in the news of the day, thereby making ourselves vulnerable to negative feelings such as anxiety and irritability. The twenty-four-hour news cycle is based largely on sensationalistic headlines designed to keep the ratings up in order to generate more advertising revenue. Excessive exposure to news headlines negates the positive effects gained during meditation. It is all too easy to be swept away by salacious stories of Hollywood celebrities that have very little relevance to our lives. It is all too common for our perspective on life to become cynical when we are fed a steady "fast food" news diet of government corruption, corporate malfeasance, and pending financial disasters. The regular practice of meditation, coupled with the study of spiritual books, helps one to retain a balanced and calm perspective amid such ongoing turbulence.

Aristotle believed that most people are ultimately searching for happiness.[1] But how can we hope to lead a happy and peaceful life if we remain conflicted by feelings of anger, frustration, and helplessness? How can we hope to make the world a better place if our own house is not in order? Meditation should be an essential component of any spiritual discipline. Its practice helps us to remain calm and collected, even when turmoil reigns about us; it helps us to see things clearly amidst outer confusion and chaos; and, finally, it leads us to that inner temple of indescribable bliss that abides in the true Self.

Nonattachment

Sages have said that one of the essential qualities needed for leading a spiritual life is a quality of sublime nonattachment. Often this is confused with a demeanor of smug aloofness from the world or an attitude of cold indifference to the welfare of others. In the spiritual books of India, this quality of detachment is indicated by the Sanskrit word *vairāgya*. One advantage of using an unfamiliar Sanskrit term is that it may prompt the reader to pause and reflect on the meaning behind the word. In *The Way of the Disciple*, Clara Codd describes vairāgya as "the ability to stand serene and steady under all circumstances."[2] In the New Testament, one of the Beatitudes declares, "Blessed are the poor in heart" (Matt. 5:8). To interpret this statement in the light of nonattachment sheds new meaning on a familiar biblical passage, one that has often been wrongly understood in the literal sense as being an endorsement of material deprivation. Was not the "poverty" that Jesus spoke of a state of mind in which there exists no attachment to material things or to a false sense of identity based on worldly perceptions and petty, self-centered concerns?

One of the obstacles to developing nonattachment is the strong sense of likes and dislikes that so many of us harbor. If someone irritates us, it's often easier to criticize than remain serene. If we have a pleasant experience, we want to repeat that experience. If we endure an unpleasant event, it's generally easier to complain than remain philosophical. If we enjoy a singular moment of success, there may be a tendency to dwell in the past while life moves on. As long as we identify with our emotional reactions to outer circumstances, we are drifting like a boat without a rudder. When things go our way, all is right with the world. But when faced with a sudden crisis, we are tossed this way and that by the storms of life.

The Greek Stoic philosopher Epictetus had some advice that still remains relevant in today's turbulent world: "Never say of anything that I have lost it, only that I have given it back."[3] Is this not another way of saying, "Blessed are the poor in heart"? Detachment implies letting go of attitudes, memories, and opinions. Can we move gracefully from youth to old age if we insist on clinging to the past? If we are an older person, do we feel somewhat diminished in retirement because we no longer hold that high-profile job we once had? As parents, do we feel emptiness inside when our children grow up and leave the nest? Can we be thankful for the life experiences we have had—whether pleasant or painful—but be free enough to live in the present moment while not being burdened by the past?

Like a river moving downstream without pause, the events of life come and go. Each stage of our life provides special lessons for the indwelling soul. A strong sense of nonattachment allows us to navigate the ever-flowing river of life without capsizing or floundering during the inevitable storms and gales that we are sure to encounter along the way.

The Possibility of Failure

Few things define our character so much as the way we deal with failure, and anyone who tries to achieve something worthwhile in life risks failing. We can fail in countless ways, and most successful people have done so at one time or another. There is no shortage of inspirational stories about remarkable people who succeeded only after having experienced the bitter taste of defeat. We find examples in the lives of business executives, entrepreneurs, authors, artists, teachers, and those in just about any other field of human endeavor.

Failure is a distinct possibility in the spiritual life as well. It is naïve to assume that lofty motives insure the realization of one's goals. Success is not guaranteed, at least in the short run. Of course, there is one sure way to avoid failure: don't even try.

Sometimes we fail because our goal is unrealistic. If I decide to learn meditation and set an immediate goal of meditating two hours per day, what are the chances that I may not make it past, say, the first week? But if I am serious, I recalibrate my daily goal to a sensible level of fifteen to twenty minutes per day and gradually increase the amount of time as I gain proficiency.

In other cases, the goals are within our reach, but we simply don't try hard enough. This type of failure is fundamentally due to a lack of enthusiasm, an inability to sustain the necessary effort required to realize our dreams. Without enthusiasm, our spiritual aspirations may be short lived, quickly overshadowed by the pressing weight of worldly priorities. If we lack the essential ingredient of enthusiasm, we need to be brutally honest and ask ourselves how serious we are about living the spiritual life.

Then there are those cases of failure in which the goal was reasonable, the desire was strong, and a sincere and sustained effort was made. Failure occurred not because of a lack of enthusiasm or dedication but because of inherent weaknesses and limitations. A Theosophist is able to face personal failures with the knowledge that for the immortal Self there is no failure. As *The Voice of the Silence* counsels, "If thou hast tried and failed, O dauntless fighter, yet lose not courage: fight on and to the charge return again, and yet again" (vs. 272). This inspirational line encourages us to summon the courage to try again even though we have momentarily fallen. So we get up. And we try again.

A Courageous Endurance

Theosophists are familiar with H. P. Blavatsky's "The Golden Stairs,"[4] a list of precepts for living the spiritual life, one of which is "a courageous endurance of personal injustice." We often recite such lofty phrases without fully realizing their implications, without considering how we might react should a great injustice be perpetrated against us. When confronted with even *minor* injustices, we may question whether it is possible for us to live up to such high ideals in this imperfect world.

Therefore, it helps to see living examples of men and women who have translated some of these spiritual guidelines into action. Occasionally, these exemplars show up in unexpected ways.

A couple of years ago, the *Chicago Tribune* carried a front-page story describing how a forty-nine-year-old man accused of rape and sent to prison had been exonerated by new DNA evidence after being incarcerated for ten years. I found myself wondering how I would have fared had I been in that unfortunate man's shoes. Would not such an experience have left me completely embittered and full of despair?

What impressed me about the *Tribune* story was the man's reaction to this tragic injustice. Initially, he responded to the situation with bitterness and anger. What normal person wouldn't? But after spending a few years in prison, he began to find solace and healing through his religious faith. "Gradually, I let it go. I put it in the

Creator's hands and I became at peace with my surroundings."5 Although he continued the legal fight to prove his innocence, this man found inner peace before he knew that DNA evidence would exonerate him. He endured years of incarceration with gentle grace and unrelenting courage.

This man may not be familiar with H. P. Blavatsky or "The Golden Stairs," but I think HPB6 would be proud of him.

Knowledge and Wisdom, Part 1

When engaged in casual conversation, we often use the words *knowledge* and *wisdom* interchangeably, but this is often due to a habit of carelessness when it comes to language. To consider these terms as being synonymous is to indulge in fuzzy thinking. *Knowledge* may be defined as "facts or ideas gained through observation, study, or experience." It also can mean "an understanding of an art, science, or technique." A definition of *wisdom* is a bit more elusive, but this should not lead us to presume that it does not exist. Philosophers throughout the ages have considered the attainment of wisdom to be the supreme goal of human existence.

To illustrate how wisdom differs from knowledge, we might begin by stating the obvious, namely, that in today's world there is a growing surplus of knowledge accompanied by a disturbing deficit of wisdom. Thanks to the Internet, we have more information at our fingertips than ever before in the history of the world. Unfortunately, examples of wisdom from leaders in all walks of life seem difficult to find.

Then there is the fact that knowledge is often a type of commodity, in the sense that it can be bought and sold, passed from teacher to seeker, from parents to children, from one generation to the next. Can you do that with wisdom? You may be as wise as Solomon, but can you transfer your wisdom to another? We can transmit ideas, distribute facts, and share statistics, but wisdom is not to be treated as a commodity that is exchanged or bartered in the marketplace. As the American patriot Thomas Paine observed, "Wisdom is not the purchase of a day."[7]

In short, knowledge has a price while wisdom is priceless. Of course, we need to acquire knowledge of various kinds, but what is most needed in this world of seemingly endless crises is the ability to link the knowledge we have with the wisdom we lack. In a pertinent passage from H. P. Blavatsky's *The Voice of the Silence*, we are reminded that "even ignorance is better than head-learning with no Soul-Wisdom to illuminate or guide it" (vs. 112).

Knowledge and Wisdom, Part 2

You've heard the clichés about the marriage counselor who's going through a divorce or the financial advisor who's filing for bankruptcy. We continue to smile at caricatures such as these because they are based on an undeniable truth: human beings don't always practice what they preach. To wit, knowledge acquired doesn't always translate into knowledge applied.

This brings us to the relationship between knowledge and wisdom. One of the interesting differences between them might be the extent to which either of them fundamentally changes who we are as a person. It should be evident, for example, that merely acquiring technical knowledge—i.e., knowing how to program a computer or analyze DNA samples—has little to do with a person's character. What is less apparent is that merely reading books on spirituality will not transform one into a likeness of St. Francis of Assisi overnight. While gaining knowledge pertaining to the spiritual life is important, true wisdom comes from the mindful application of that knowledge to our daily actions.

The Voice of the Silence offers this simple but enduring advice: "Be humble, if thou would'st attain to wisdom" (vs. 161). When we are overly conscious of our intellectual achievements, we create a subtle impediment to the attainment of wisdom. An eighteenth-century English poet, William Cowper, put it this way: "Knowledge is proud that he has learned so much; wisdom is humble that he knows no more."[8] His Holiness the 14th Dalai Lama, for example, may know as much about Tibetan Buddhism as any living scholar, but his genuine sense of humility is never overshadowed by his vast amount of learning.

We can compartmentalize and isolate our knowledge from the way we live our daily life, but our wisdom, never. A scholar may possess an impressive intellectual inventory within his chosen field of study and still be prone to selfishness, jealousy, and other defects of character. In his book *Seeking Wisdom*, Theosophical author N. Sri Ram summed it up this way: "When we try to understand the nature of wisdom, we will find that we cannot separate it from life."[9]

Knowledge and Wisdom, Part 3

In these current times, millions of people are obsessed with celebrity culture. Witness the popularity of the New York and London tabloids, the ubiquitous, self-promoting video clips found on YouTube, and the mindless tweets sent out on Twitter by celebrities to their legions of followers. It's no secret that celebrities sometimes behave foolishly, nor is it surprising that a large segment of the public derives voyeuristic enjoyment from observing the antics of the rich and famous.

By way of contrast, the Mahatmas of the wisdom tradition are probably the ultimate antithesis of today's typical celebrity. Shunning the media spotlight, the Mahatmas quietly carry out their important work in anonymity. Among other things, they are said to possess profound wisdom. Have you ever pondered the attributes of a wise person? Over two thousand years ago, a warrior named Arjuna once did just that. In the second chapter of the Bhagavad Gita, he asked his charioteer, Krishna, "What are the characteristics of the sage who possesses ever calm wisdom? . . . How does this sage of steady wisdom speak and sit and walk?"[10]

Although he lived centuries after the writing of the Bhagavad Gita, the Roman statesman and writer Cicero knew the answer to Arjuna's question. In his essay "On the Good Life," Cicero wrote, "The wise man is free from all those disturbances of the soul which I describe as passions; his heart is full of tranquil calm forever."[11]

Knowledge alone will not quiet our restless hearts, nor will it provide the peace we so desperately seek in this troubled world. If peace of heart and mind were simply a function of more knowledge, anybody with a PhD would be living a life of uninterrupted serenity.

Oliver Wendell Homes once said, "It is the province of knowledge to speak, and it is the privilege of wisdom to listen."[12] Have you noticed that a wise person is not overly talkative? More often than not they remain silent, while others tend to speak without weighing the effects and consequences of their words.

Whereas knowledge comes from without, wisdom arises from within, and its presence is facilitated by our ability to rise above our personal nature and engage in periods of quiet reflection and introspection.

The Task at Hand

One of the central challenges faced by many people today is how to remain focused on the task at hand. The ability to concentrate the mind for a period of time—without interruptions, without distractions—is essential to the accomplishment of anything of value. Whether one is an engineer or an artist, a detective or a playwright, the ability consciously to direct the movements of the mind is crucial to achievement.

Some people find it easier than others to inhibit the wandering tendencies of the mind, but even those with a natural facility for sustained mental concentration are bound to be challenged by the conditions of our technological world. The temptations that divert and seduce our attention are endless, especially those arising from cyberspace. Perhaps more than in any previous age, constant distraction and fickleness of thought are endemic to the popular culture of our time. While the Internet has provided us with many wonderful resources, it also brings problems. In 1947, the economist Herbert A. Simon noted, "A wealth of information creates a poverty of attention."[13] How prescient his comment seems today! With the mind of an accountant, accustomed to dealing with ledgers and balance sheets, Simon knew instinctively that a surplus of X leads to a deficit of Y.

Each of us is here for a purpose; at least, many of us believe that to be the case. Our time in this incarnation is limited; of this there can be no debate. The question then arises: What are we doing with our allotted time? Dante placed those souls who had committed the sin of prodigality in the fourth circle of his *Inferno*. To be prodigious is to be wasteful, to squander one's resources. Money is a resource, but so is time. Money lost can be earned again, while time lost is a nonrecoverable asset. Like many others, I have lost (or wasted) both money and time. As I get older and the inevitable but unknown time of my departure from this world approaches, the loss of the former bothers me less and less, while my foolish misuse of the latter brings pangs of regret.

A Conscious Surrendering

In Madame Blavatsky's spiritual guidebook, *The Voice of the Silence,* the disciple is warned of the "great dire heresy" (vs. 37). This refers to the common delusion that the personal self exists separately from the universal Self, from which all life flows. The spiritual amnesia that accompanies embodiment in physical form brings about identification with the temporal self and a forgetfulness of our true nature. In this respect, one is like an actor, so immersed in the role to be played that he becomes, for the moment, that character. As aspirants to the spiritual life, it is our task to rise above the temporal self and realize our fundamental identity with the One. In *The Light of Asia,* Sir Edwin Arnold describes this sublime experience as the moment when "the dewdrop slips into the shining sea."[14]

There is a parallel, I think, between this merging of the particular consciousness with the universal and that of the artist working under the sway of inspiration. In an article entitled "Tradition and the Individual Talent," T. S. Eliot describes the creative process of the writer as one in which the writer steps outside of himself, so to speak, and becomes a channel for something greater and more enduring. "What happens is a continual surrender of himself, as he is at the moment, to something which is more valuable. The process of an artist is a continual self-sacrifice, a continual extinction of personality."[15]

With both the aspirant and the artist, there is a conscious surrendering of the personal self. This willing relinquishment can result in an influx of vibrant energy and a wonderful sense of freedom unlike anything one may experience when hampered by the limitations of the personal ego. The supreme goal put before the aspirant in such guidebooks as *The Voice of the Silence* is to be of service. With the artist, the creative process is generally described as one of self-expression; that may be accurate, but it is not the whole story. When one considers the relation of art to society, there is also the element of service. Enduring art of high quality is a gift to the world. In referring to the poet William Butler Yeats—who was well acquainted with Theosophy—T. S. Eliot said, "[He] showed that an artist, by serving his art with entire integrity, is at the same time rendering the greatest service he can to his own nation and to the whole world."[16]

Chapter 5

CONTEMPORARY ISSUES

The Power of Ideas

How little do we know that which we are! How less what we may be!

—Lord Byron, *Don Juan, Canto 15*

Plato is credited with saying that ideas rule the world. In his book *The History of a Crime* (1877), the French novelist and dramatist Victor Hugo observed, "There is one thing stronger than all the armies in the world; and that is an idea whose time has come." As students of Theosophy, we should have a special understanding of the power of thought.

Conventional thinking states that reality is that which can be touched, weighed, and measured—in short, the tangible world around us. Thought and ideas are acknowledged as having significance, but the materialist views them as *derivative*—not primary. In other words, they are byproducts of neurological processes taking place within the physical organ of the brain.

The Theosophist, on the other hand, turns the conventional scientific view on its head by declaring that it is *ideas* that are *primary*, while the *world* is *derivative*. In *The Secret Doctrine*, for instance, we read that "the Universe was evolved out of its ideal plan" (1:281) and that "the Universe is worked and *guided*, from *within outwards*" (1:274). This physical world, which seems so real to us, has been found by modern physicists to be nothing more than a phantom, an illusion of the senses. This seemingly solid matter consists of tiny molecules, which in turn consist of smaller atoms, which in turn consist of subatomic particles, all of which seem to resemble a *mental construct* rather than the ultimate building block of nature posited by scientists in the nineteenth century.

In other words, the substratum of the universe appears to be a thought.

But our society has been increasingly influenced by the materialistic point of view: the universe is a random occurrence and the existence of human life (or any life form) is an "accident." This attitude has led to a growing malaise of hopelessness and futility on the part of many. What is now needed is recognition of the fact that our lives have purpose and that we live in an ordered and intelligent universe.

Emerson said, "The key to every man is his thought."[1] Let us recognize the creative power of thought and the crucial role it plays in remaking our world. We are not victims, pawns, or "accidents" of blind evolutionary forces. We are intelligent beings endowed with the divine power of creative thought.

A Casualty of the Information Age?

Where is the wisdom we have lost in knowledge?
Where is the knowledge we have lost in information?

—T. S. ELIOT, *THE ROCK*

We live in the so-called information age. Satellite and cable TV now provide a plethora of channels, whereas our grandparents somehow survived on only a handful of stations. The Internet allows us to scan the London *Times*, the *New York Times*, or virtually any newspaper around the world at the click of a mouse. *Publishers Weekly* reports that over 687 million books were sold in 2017, an increase from 674 million in 2016. While driving our car, we can listen to NPR, AP News, and a variety of talk shows from sports to gardening, from politics to investing. At home and in the office we receive a daily deluge of emails from friends, colleagues, and strangers. Where does it all end? And who has time to deal with all of it?

The glut of information provided by today's technology can easily overwhelm us if we are not careful. The practical person may wonder, "How much information do I really need?" The thoughtful person might ask, "What are the consequences of indiscriminately filling my mind with endless media chatter?" The Theosophist inquires, "Does this historically unprecedented access to information hinder or help my spiritual quest?"

These are questions that we have to answer for ourselves. We have to discover our own limits and vulnerabilities to the relentless media barrage, and we can do so only by careful self-observation in which we become aware of how the kaleidoscope of data affects our inner life. Are we able to remain centered and serene under most circumstances, or have we become agitated and distracted? Are we in touch with the spiritual side of life, or have we allowed our mind to become a playground for useless and frivolous sound bites?

Theosophical literature provides some valuable guidelines that can help us navigate this endless sea of information. For instance, *At the Feet of the Master* tells us to discriminate between "the important and the unimportant, the useful and the useless."[2] *The Voice of the Silence* advises us to discern "the ever-fleeting from the ever-lasting" (vs. 111). *Light on the Path* offers this paradoxical advice: "Listen only to the voice which is soundless."[3] If much of today's media noise is inconsequential, ephemeral, and abrasively loud, what does that tell us?

To live a spiritual life, we need to be capable of experiencing deep inner stillness. To live our life wisely, we need time for quiet and thoughtful reflection. It will be difficult to experience inner peace and intuitive insights if our minds are consuming a constant and steady diet of media chatter. As the poetry of T. S. Eliot suggests, the loss of wisdom in this superficial and frenzied technological era may be the ultimate casualty of the information age.

Digital Distraction

When the season of Lent approaches, many Christians consider what type of sacrifice they will make to remember the forty days that Jesus is said to have wandered in the wilderness. As a sign of the times, *The Wall Street Journal* reported recently that some Christians are vowing to exit the digital wilderness of social-networking sites for the Lenten season. While online sites such a Facebook and MySpace are immensely popular with young people, it appears that a significant percentage of adults also regularly frequent such sites. Some of these adults admit that it has become a mild form of addiction, as they log on twenty to thirty times a day to contact their hundreds of "friends."

The word *acquaintances* might be a more accurate, although less flattering, description for the people on those lists of names. Most thoughtful people realize that when you dilute a word such as *friend* by a factor of 200 or 300, that word no longer bears any resemblance to its original meaning. Aristotle observes that true friendship is a rare blessing, something to be cherished and maintained throughout the course of one's life. In book 8 of the *Nicomachean Ethics*, he lists three general kinds of friendship: The first kind is based on utility and, being based on mutual gain, is relatively impermanent, changing according to circumstances. The second kind is based on pleasure. Aristotle notes that this kind is prevalent among the young, as their lives are regulated largely by their mercurial feelings. These friendships come to an end when tastes change and pleasures are no longer shared in common. The third kind of friendship is based on goodness, or virtuous conduct.

Aristotle praises this as the highest type, because it is based not on personal gain or selfish pleasure but on true caring for the well-being of another person.[4]

Those who have a few such friendships in their life may consider themselves fortunate. Aristotle recognizes the value of the other two categories, but he places a premium on the third type, which often lasts a lifetime or, as Theosophists might believe, several lifetimes. H. P. Blavatsky once said that we are "ceaselessly self-deceived" by our own ignorance. Digital technology offers much to enhance the quality of our lives, but, like a double-edged sword, it also has the capacity for endless distraction to those ensnared by the cult of personality.

Are You Connected?

The statement known as the Theosophical Worldview contains these words: "The universe and all that exists within it are one interrelated and interdependent whole." These are potent words and worthy of prolonged meditation. To the extent that we realize this sublime truth, our lives become increasingly grounded in a deeper reality. But any good idea taken to excess becomes problematic. As one of the Masters of Wisdom wrote: "Evil is the exaggeration of the good."[5]

Being connected is a big part of today's popular culture. Communication technology allows people to interact in new and exciting ways that could hardly have been imagined by earlier generations. This is all to the good, but sometimes a good thing taken to excess turns out being not so good after all.

An article from the archives of *The Christian Science Monitor* points to a disturbing and growing phenomenon of the information age. David Shenk, author of *Data Smog,* is quoted as saying that people are suffering from "a nonstop orgy of connectedness that can sometimes crowd out tenderness and meaning."[6] Modern technology has brought us many marvels for which we can be thankful, yet there is a fine line between *using* technology and *being used* by technology. If you feel compelled to log on to Facebook or MySpace twenty times a day, you may need to ask yourself if you are connected or just plain distracted.

Obviously, the statement of interconnectedness as expressed in the Theosophical Worldview is referring to something very different. It is all about establishing deep communion with the divine Source through a sustained program of contemplation and meditation. To be in touch with the outer world is obviously necessary in order to function, but dwelling too much on the peripherals of life weakens our spiritual foundations. It's a matter of balance. There is a striking passage in the thirteenth chapter of the Bhaghavad Gita that speaks to the current issue of information overload in our society. In that chapter, Lord Krishna is speaking to the warrior Arjuna about "that which ought to be known."[7] In today's increasingly plugged-in world, the spiritual aspirant might do well to stop occasionally and reflect on what is really worth knowing.

To Be Everywhere Is to Be Nowhere

In my younger days, my voracious appetite for reading drove me to purchase books that I intended to read but somehow never did, books that would end up sitting on my bookshelf for years, collecting dust and taking up space, for it always seemed easier finding the money to buy the books than finding the time to read them. All too often I walked out of a bookstore weighing ten pounds more than when I strolled in. It wasn't that I didn't like to read. In fact, the opposite was the problem. I had far too many books and only a limited amount of time.

Does any of that sound familiar?

Then one day, while reading a book by Annie Besant, I came across some very useful advice:

In one way, the multitude of books that we have at the present day is a disadvantage. It induces reading without thinking, which produces superficiality and fickleness of thought. That is why I always advise people to read a little and then reproduce what they have read, not by memory, but out of the clear grasp of the subject that they have obtained. Only what you have thought out is really yours, and only by thinking over and understanding what you read and hear, can you make it your own."[8]

I've tried taking that advice to heart, reading fewer books but spending more time on books of substance, pausing frequently to reflect, consider, and question, and then attempting to recapitulate the author's main ideas using my own words.

Seneca, a first-century Roman statesman and philosopher, seems to be on the same page as Annie Besant. He is remembered for his writings on Stoic philosophy and particularly for his *Letters*, all of which enjoyed resurgence in popularity during the European Renaissance. In one of the letters, he offers some advice to a friend who was given to spending too much time with books:

People who spend their whole life traveling abroad end up having plenty of places where they can find hospitality but no real friendships. The same must needs be the case with people who never set about acquiring an intimate acquaintanceship with any one great writer, but skip from one to another, paying flying visits to them all.[9]

I think Seneca had it right . . . but then he never walked into a megabookstore.

Our Interconnected World

To observe that our world has become smaller is as unremarkable as it is undeniable. We've all experienced this smallness in so many ways: a devastating tsunami galvanizes instant aid from countries thousands of miles away; a falling US dollar influences the monetary policies of central bankers in Europe and Brazil; the unexpected death of celebrity chef Anthony Bourdain shocks millions of fans the world over. A few centuries ago, a person living in North America had little reason to worry about events in Europe; the average European gave little thought to China; and China remained an insular nation, largely unconcerned with the scientific and social advances made in the West. All this has changed. No longer can any nation afford to adopt an isolationist posture in an age of global communications. Human beings the world over are inexorably becoming more connected.

The principle of interconnectedness is a basic Theosophical principle, as this excerpt from the Theosophical Worldview shows:

> The universe and all that exists within it are one interrelated and interdependent whole. Every existent being—from atom to galaxy—is rooted in the same universal, life-creating Reality.[10]

The full implications of this statement are profound, going much deeper than the obvious examples given above. It's easy to find examples of cause and effect operating in the outer world, but we have yet to fully understand how interconnected we are in the inner realms.

By virtue of our common humanity, we are deeply connected, not only at the material level but also at the level of thought. Whether we live in Brazil, China, Europe, or the United States, we are connected at those deeper levels where thought and feeling operate. When our ideas are published in books or periodicals, they can influence the reader, but even our private and unspoken thoughts radiate energy outwardly, having their proportionate effect upon the surrounding mental atmosphere. Annie Besant summed this truth up at the 1893 World Parliament of Religions in Chicago: "Even as you think, the thought burning in your brain becomes a living force for good or for evil in the mental atmosphere. As a man thinks, thoughts from him go out to mould the thoughts and lives of other men. Your thought power makes you creative gods in the world."[11]

Intellectual Brilliance and Spiritual Blindness

There are those who believe the universe to be nothing more than a random occurrence, the result of blind evolutionary forces, devoid of purpose and meaning. Some of the advocates for the material-istic doctrine are quite brilliant—Stephen Hawkings, for example. But intellectual brilliance is sometimes accompanied by spiritual blindness. A worldview that depicts the universe as a mindless dance of atoms, molecules, and subatomic particles is not one that inspires or uplifts the human spirit. Its message is cold, sterile, and nihilistic. For those who respect science but recoil at the idea that the universe is nothing more than the result of a big cosmic sneeze, Theosophy has something to offer.

Theosophical teachings point to a divine plan in which every sentient being plays its part. No form of life is without significance, however lowly it may appear to be. Animating the vast expanse of our universe is the One Life, expressing itself through countless forms, all of which are evolving along their particular evolution-ary path. Moreover, the universe is governed by law, not incoherent and random probabilities. On this point, Blavatsky, in *The Secret Doctrine*, is quite clear: "There is a purpose in every important act of Nature" (1:640). Moreover, the scope of the divine plan is not limited to our Earth: "There are millions and millions of worlds and firmaments visible to us; there are still greater numbers beyond those visible to the telescopes, and many of the latter kind do not belong to our *objective* sphere of existence" (1:605). What is presented in modern Theosophical literature is only a small portion of the divine plan; undoubtedly there is much that remains a mystery.

The materialist will reply that life has no inherent purpose, that any attempt to discover meaning is driven by our psychological needs or insecurities. But the thirst for meaning is too deeply rooted in human nature for that cynical explanation to hold true. To live a life devoid of meaning is to live without light. As Tennyson said in his poem "The Higher Pantheism," "Dark is the world to thee; thyself are the reason why." The fact that many great minds continue to reflect upon the purpose of life suggests that at some level there exists an awareness that life *does* have a purpose. Our lives would be infinitely more satisfying and fulfilling if we sensed that there is a deep purpose to our being here, not to mention that this would enable us to endure hardships and setbacks with equanimity. I think that most thoughtful people would prefer that kind of a life to a comfortable and uneventful one without any sense of purpose whatsoever.

Why Johnny Can't Meditate

In the East, the tendency of the mind to wander has long been recognized as an impediment to making progress in the spiritual life. For example, Patanjali states in the *Yoga Sutras* that "Yoga is the inhibition of the modifications of the mind."[12] The term *modification* refers to the natural inclination of the mind to engage in restless and perpetual movement. In the *Viveka-Cūdūmani*, Shankaracharya lists the qualification of *samādhāna*—the ability to avoid idle thoughts while focusing the mind solely on Truth or Brahman.[13] In more recent times, Krishnamurti tells us in *At the Feet of the Master* that we should develop the quality of one-pointedness by giving our full attention to whatever task is at hand.[14]

Modernity tends to equate progress largely with advances made in science and technology. Ironically, some of those advances are what make it so difficult to achieve the mental habit of one-pointedness. Due to the relentless encroachment of technology into every facet of our lives, we are faced with a growing number of attractive distractions that spiritual aspirants of earlier times never had to face.

One of the main culprits is the Internet. In his book *The Shallows: What the Internet Is Doing to Our Brains*, Nicholas Carr describes the problem: "Dozens of studies by psychologists, neurobiologists, educators, and Web designers point to the same conclusion: when we go online, we enter an environment that promotes cursory reading, hurried and distracted thinking, and superficial learning."[15]

Think about it. The typical Web page is filled with ads, pop-ups, videos, and embedded hot links—all serving to disperse our attention as though it were a steel ball in a pinball machine.

Carr continues: "Psychological research long ago proved what most of us know from experience: frequent interruptions scatter our thoughts, weaken our memory, and make us tense and anxious."[16] Is it any coincidence that attention spans seem to be shrinking?

The reality is that the Internet is not going away and that technology will continue to innovate. We can use technology for its many benefits, but we should also be aware of its potential to impact our state of mind in a negative way. If Patanjali or Shankaracharya were living today, they would undoubtedly make use of our current amazing technology. At the same time, they would also instruct their students to turn off their cell phones and electronic devices from time to time in order to develop concentration and one-pointedness. The choice for us is clear: we can use technology, or it will use us.

Silence: An Endangered Species

Isn't it strange how sometimes you can forget the name of a movie you saw last weekend or what you had for dinner before the movie, while certain events from the distant past remain embedded in your memory like the Rock of Gibraltar?

I have this indelible memory of a rare moment of overpowering silence, the likes of which I had never before experienced. The year was 1970 when, as part of the Third Infantry Division of the US Army, I was stationed in South Korea. One of my weekend walks had taken me into a remote rural area, far from the base and far from any roads or highways. The noise of trucks, taxis, and other city sounds had long since faded away. Across a distant rice paddy, a farmer walked slowly beside an ox that was pulling a wooden cart. They made no sound and appeared not to be in any hurry. I remember thinking that this iconic scene could have easily taken place one thousand years ago, in a time long before the noisy industrialized era. It is hard to describe, but the silence had an overpowering quality to it, and it touched me deeply.

Just as we need sunlight and water for physical health and survival, we also require periodic silence to maintain our spiritual health. In Psalm 46 we find the commandment, "Be still and know that I am God." In *Light on the Path* we read, "Listen only to the voice which is soundless."[17] But in today's world, random sounds are ubiquitous, and silence is a rarity. Everywhere you go—the gas station, the grocery store, the office—and even at home, you are assaulted by indiscriminate waves of sound as they invade your personal space, impinge on your consciousness, and demand your attention.

In *One Square Inch of Silence: One Man's Search for Silence in a Noisy World*, Gordon Hempton, an acoustic ecologist, warns, "Today silence has become an endangered species. Our cities, our suburbs, our farm communities, even our most expensive and remote national parks are not free from human noise intrusions."[18] All this underscores the necessity to establish room for silence in our busy lives. Today, when one is accosted at every turn by a cacophony of strident sounds and enervating dissonance, the need for silence is a matter of both mental and spiritual well-being. That South Korean rice paddy, in which I experienced that extraordinary moment of serenity some forty years ago, has probably given way to a paved highway and the mechanized sounds of modern civilization. The outer world is what it is. But through quiet reflection and regular meditative practices, we can create our own inner sanctuary of silence, regardless of what is going on in the world around us.

Chapter 6

REINCARNATION

A Common Objection to Reincarnation

How can reincarnation be true in light of the world's population explosion? People sometimes raise this question based on the assumption that we are reborn immediately after dying. Given that the earth's population has increased from one billion to over six billion in a mere two hundred years, what accounts for all the new souls being born?

First, we should note that the belief that our planet's population will continue to grow unchecked—an idea that gained acceptance in the 1960s—is being questioned by current world-census studies. In many developed countries, the fertility rates have dropped to the point where populations are shrinking. Russia[1] and France[2] now offer financial incentives for young women to have more children. In underdeveloped countries, the population continues to grow, but the rate of growth is dropping. Recent estimates now predict the global population will reach a plateau around 2050.

Irrespective of prognostications by world-census takers, how *does* one reconcile the idea of reincarnation with the population explosion? According to Theosophical wisdom, the time between death and rebirth varies from a few hundred years to a thousand or more. If the pool of available souls for our globe is, say, sixty billion, roughly 10 percent are incarnated at this time. Therefore, the population growth of the past two hundred years would not have had to depend on the arrival of "new" souls.

The question then becomes, why are so many souls being reborn in these modern times? Here's a possible answer. In centuries past, life moved at a slower pace. Perhaps you lived in ancient Egypt and were reborn there again after a few hundred years. A new pyramid might have been erected, a new dynasty perhaps; yet life in general would not have dramatically changed. But with the advance of modern science, the advent of the industrial revolution, and now the arrival of the information age, life moves at a pace unimaginable to those ancient Egyptians. At the level of the personal self, it can be very stressful to live in such times as we do. On the other hand, periods of dramatic political, cultural, and social upheavals may provide tremendous opportunities for evolutionary growth of the immortal soul—the advance of such evolution being the precise purpose of reincarnation in the first place, according to Theosophy.

The increase in global population is, therefore, a phenomenon that is not necessarily incompatible with the Theosophical view of reincarnation.

Reincarnation and Past-Life Memories

One of the more common objections to the idea of reincarnation is the inability of most people to recall past-life memories. "If I have lived former lives, why is it that I cannot remember any of them?" This response is predictable and easily addressed.

The short answer is that nature does not necessarily intend for us to recall our past lives. Imagine the psychological weight of carrying vivid memories of our past limitations, disappointments, and failures from former incarnations. Imagine the debilitating guilt accompanying the conscious awareness of previous acts of injury, betrayal, and malfeasance, had we, in fact, committed such acts. Burdened with this handicap, cynicism and despair would be the natural inclination of youth, not optimism and hope. Fortunately, nature shows herself to be both wise and beneficent by blocking conscious access to the past-life ledger that catalogues our deeds and misdeeds of former lives. Those memories are no more necessary in this present life than it is for an actor presently engaged in playing a part in Hamlet to remember lines from a previous performance of Othello.

Theosophy teaches that such memories are retained by the soul in what Theosophy refers to as the *causal body*. The causal vehicle is the repository of the distilled wisdom gained by our personalities through a long series of deaths and rebirths. Although such memories normally cannot be recalled by the brain consciousness, they do manifest in a given life as specific abilities, talents, and inclinations—or what we might call *indirect* memories. Direct memory recalls the specific details of a past event, whether it occurred two hours ago or two years ago. Indirect memory recalls only the lessons learned from past experience. Even within the span of a single lifetime, we demonstrate certain skills while forgetting the mechanics of how we acquired them. For example, a concert pianist does not need to remember the endless hours of repetition spent practicing scales and chords in order to perform splendidly onstage before a live audience. An experienced actor does not need to remember the plot, character, and lines from roles performed years ago in order to perform brilliantly today in a brand-new role. In the same way, we do not need to recall the countless details of our past lives in order to employ the wisdom, skills, and capacities built up within the causal body over a long series of reincarnations.

None of this is meant to suggest that authentic past-life memories are nonexistent. Some people do claim to remember something of their previous lives. The fascinating work of the late Dr. Ian

Stevenson of the University of Virginia offers ample evidence to
support such claims, especially as it has been exhibited in hundreds of cases involving young children around the world.[3] But
the plausibility of reincarnation as a viable theory does not suffer
because we are unable to retrieve memories of our former lives.

Dreams Are Forever

Have perseverance as one who doth for evermore endure (vs. 138).

How does a person remain an optimist despite having endured
repeated setbacks and even outright failure while attempting to
realize his or her innermost dreams? Once the vibrancy of youth
begins to fade and the years go by, how does one maintain the
enthusiasm and drive needed to pursue one's goals despite the obstacles and endless distractions?

For Theosophists, who tend to view life from a wider perspective, all such failures are only temporary. A person sees this lifetime
as one of many, and the important thing is to keep striving, to
continue working toward the realization of one's highest potential.
In particular, the knowledge of reincarnation provides the basis
whereby our unfulfilled dreams and aspirations will have yet another opportunity to reach fruition. "Each sincere attempt wins its
reward in time," says *The Voice of the Silence* (vs. 274).

The amateur writer who never quite finished her first novel
has nevertheless laid the foundation for future lives when the creative impulse will surface once again. The aspiring concert pianist
whose technique was not quite up to Carnegie Hall standards has
nevertheless nurtured a powerful desire to express himself through
music, and the momentum of that effort is not lost when his present life draws to a close. Spiritual aspirants who struggle daily with
the limitations of their personal nature may at times succumb to

materialism or egotism, but, from the standpoint of the immortal Self, such regressions are only temporary setbacks on the long path to eventual Self-Realization.

The Voice of the Silence provides some poignant words of encouragement for all sincere aspirants: "If thou hast tried and failed, O dauntless fighter, yet lose not courage; fight on and to the charge return again, and yet again" (vs. 272). If we lived only one brief lifetime on this earth, such fine sounding words would be of limited value. However, an understanding of reincarnation allows us to take such words of encouragement to heart and to enter life's busy arena once more with renewed optimism, confidence, and vigor.

Why Don't We Remember Our Past Lives?

Although my mother taught me the concept of reincarnation when I was a child, I never spent much time wondering about my past lives. A Sufi dancer once told me that I had once been a female dancer in India and another time a priest in Africa. Due to my affinity for all things Japanese, my wife is convinced that my last incarnation was in Japan, and she may be right. While I recognize that some people may derive therapeutic value in undergoing past-life regressions, I've never felt the urge to know whether I'd been cast as "a puppet, a pauper, a pirate, a poet, a pawn and a king"[4] in any of my past lives. This present role is fascinating and challenging enough.

But for many inquirers, the question remains: If reincarnation is a fact, why *don't* we remember our past lives? Would it not be useful to recall the details—or at least a summary—of our previous appearances upon this terrestrial stage? A reasonable response to these queries is given by Sri Madhava Ashish:

> If there were no barrier between [past life memories] and our present conscious integrations, we would be compelled, like trams, to

follow the same old tracks of thought and behavior worn by the sum of our previous lives, each time wearing the grooves a little deeper. Our past inadequacies would crush us, our past glories would inflate us. It is enough to know that all that has ever happened has made us what we are, and that all that we ever were is present in us now. We do not need to know the details of past lives, for each life is, up to a point, a recapitulation of all our previous lives.[5]

When a professional actor takes on a new role, the character and the plot and the script from the previous performance are forgotten. What is not discarded are the acting skills honed through numerous theatrical performances. So it is with each of us as we repeatedly return to the earthly stage, life after life, in a new setting and with a new personality. The important thing to know is that throughout these cycles of birth and death, we endure as the immortal Actor and not the fleeting roles in which we are temporarily cast.

The Fear of Death

For many people, the study of Theosophy has alleviated the fear of death. When my father, a lifelong Theosophist, was lying in a hospital after a severe stroke, I felt the need to ask him if he was afraid of dying. Although he was a quiet man who kept things to himself, I wanted to take that opportunity to find out what was in his heart. His reply was both immediate and reassuring. With a trace of a smile, he gently shook his head from side to side, indicating that death held no trepidation for him. It was such a natural response that I had no reason to doubt him. A few days later he passed over to the other side.

The Roman philosopher Marcus Tullius Cicero, in his later years, wrote the now-famous essay "On Old Age." Written in the

style of the Platonic dialogues, its popularity has endured throughout the·centuries; both US president John Adams and Benjamin
Franklin were admirers of this timeless essay. In one remarkable
passage, Cicero uses a maritime simile to describe his feelings
about death: "As I approach death I feel like a man nearing harbor
after a long voyage: I seem to be catching sight of land."[6]

At the moment of birth, each soul embarks upon a voyage, one
that is sometimes turbulent or foreboding, while at other times
placid and serene. We have navigated this sea before, although we
know it not. But whether our journey is barren or fruitful, hasty
or prolonged, one thing is certain—at some point our tired vessel
will return to the harbor and we will disembark.

When death beckons at the end of a long life, its arrival is
often presaged by a sense that the journey has run its course.
Faintly catching a glimpse of the shoreline through the seaborne
haze, we are as the wayfarer who left port ages ago and now
returns home. Then, just like Tennyson's Ulysses, we may trium-
phantly exclaim: "Much have I seen and known . . . I am a part
of all I have met."[7]

The River of Forgetfulness

Anyone who has seriously thought about reincarnation has probably wondered about their past lives. *Who was I? What did I do?
Where did I live?*

The River Lethe of Greek mythology, one of the five rivers
flowing through Hades, is associated with the spirit of forgetfulness and oblivion. This symbol is found in the last section of
Plato's *Republic,* where souls are required to drink from the River
of Forgetfulness before returning to earthly life; in Virgil's *Aeneid,*
where drinking the waters is said to "quench man's troubles [with]
the deep draught of oblivion"[8]; and in Seneca's *Hercules Furens,* in

which Lethe is described as a placid stream that has the power to take away our earthly cares.[9]

But what if we *could* recall our former lives? Wouldn't that prove to be of great value? Wouldn't that knowledge serve to guide us through life's challenges and difficulties? Listen to what N. Sri Ram has to say:

> It is a mercy that we are able to start each time—each incarnation—fresh-bathed in the waters of Lethe, in oblivious innocence. Each time we draw back into ourselves, in order to put ourselves out into the external world to greater advantage. The slate is wiped clean that we may draw upon it a more perfect picture. If we had to draw upon a slate already filled with innumerable and indelible characters, we would be running the certain risk of making confusion worse confounded, until we were hopelessly lost in a morass of memories, bitter and sweet, breeding remorse and re-awakening passions, at best a bewilderment, more likely a nightmare.[10]

The reincarnating Self has been compared to an actor who is called on to play different roles. His or her creative abilities and powers of expression grow with each role. During the actual performance, however, the particulars of all previous performances must be forgotten. The actor's mind is focused solely on the character at hand. And so it is with the higher Self, as it enters each new incarnation with increased powers and capacities born of experience but without being burdened by memories of the distant past.

Chapter 7

QUESTIONS TO CONTEMPLATE

The Infinite Bosom of Duration

"Time was not, for it lay asleep in the infinite bosom of duration." This enigmatic verse from the Stanzas of Dzyan[1] attempts to describe "the state of the ONE ALL during Pralaya, before the first flutter of reawakening manifestation."[2] The language employed throughout stanza one reverberates with mystical overtones; it soon becomes evident to the first-time reader that a literal interpretation of the verses is totally inappropriate. What is also evident is that this particular verse suggests a mysterious relationship between time and duration.

We are familiar with chronological time, which is delineated by seconds, hours, days, and years. These demarcations of time are objective and therefore predictable. Psychological time, however, is subjective and thus unpredictable. A person bored with a lecture may feel time crawling at a turtle's pace, while the next person may be enthused by the speaker and therefore have a sense that time has passed by rather quickly. Measured by the clock, the time of the lecture is the same for both listeners, but their subjective sense of time could hardly be more different.

The book *Transactions of the Blavatsky Lodge* recounts H. P. Blavatsky being asked the following question by a Theosophist attending a meeting: "What is the difference between Time and Duration?" She answered, "Duration *is*; it has neither beginning nor end. Duration is beginningless and endless; Time is finite."[3]

As creatures with finite bodies, we have an intimate knowledge of time, whether in the chronological or psychological sense. But what about the eternal Duration mentioned in the Stanzas of Dzyan? Is there something within us capable of understanding, or responding to, eternal Duration? Is there some aspect of our Being that is without beginning and without end?

There is a memorable line in *The Voice of the Silence*, which suggests that the answer to these questions is affirmative: "Thy shadows live and vanish; that which in thee shall live forever, that which in thee knows, for it is knowledge, is not of fleeting life: it is the man that was, that is, and will be, for whom the hour shall never strike" (vs. 138).

Whether we like it or not, the clock of Time ticks away relentlessly. A human being appears briefly upon the world stage and then disappears. Universes appear and then disappear. As the poet Horace queried, "What do the ravages of time not injure?"

What is that mystery within us that endures? Do we have a sense of it? Have we even tried to find it?

Coincidence, or Not?

Sometimes the confluence of two events is merely coincidence, while at other times what appears to be coincidence may be an indication of unseen forces at work. The other day, for example, my wife and I left our home to see a movie just as our neighbor was leaving. My wife and I returned three hours later; as we parked our car, we noticed that our neighbor had also returned and was parking *his* car. Was that a mere coincidence? Probably.

The next situation involves a phone call. First, some background is necessary: As the director of education at the Theosophical Society, I work with many prisoners who enroll in our correspondence courses.[4] One such prisoner—we'll call him Randy—had been working with me throughout 2007. He was a good student and always gave thoughtful answers to the study questions. Randy was released from prison in February 2008, at which time he returned to his hometown of Charlotte, North Carolina. He still kept in touch with me by phone, and I tried to encourage him in his job search. After living at the Salvation Army for a few months, he eventually found a job installing carpet. The last time I heard from Randy was in August 2008, and he was still holding down that job.

Fast forward to March 2009. I'm in the office organizing my files when I find Randy's old study papers. Why not give him a call? Seven months have passed since we last talked. For several days I consider phoning him, but work deadlines are encroaching, so I never get around to it. The following Monday morning, there's a message on my phone. It's from Randy, who has called to say hello.

Randy was seven hundred miles away, and we hadn't spoken in seven months. There was no compelling reason for either of us to contact the other. Yet, after thinking of him for a couple of days, I received a phone call from him. Is that coincidence? Or is it evidence of the "unexplained laws of nature" at work?

A False Beacon of Hope?

One hundred and fifty years ago, Charles Dickens wrote: "It was the best of times, it was the worst of times." Many of you may recognize this as the opening gambit from his *A Tale of Two Cities*. Although these words were written in 1859, historians have observed how well they served as an epithet for the entire twentieth century, an era marked by great optimism and achievement, as well as by unspeakable barbarism and depravity.

In the first chapter of *A Tale of Two Cities*, Dickens continues his use of balanced syntax: "It was the age of wisdom, it was the age of foolishness; it was the epoch of belief, it was the epoch of incredulity; it was the season of Light; it was the season of Darkness."

Will our twenty-first century be characterized by violent clashes of a similar nature? Time will tell. As we survey the present state of the world, one indicator that portends a continuation of such polar extremes is the apparent advance of technology unhinged from moral or ethical considerations. While it is undeniable that science has brought numerous benefits and improvements to human life, there is an uneasy suspicion among thoughtful observers that technology is becoming a false beacon of hope, leading us instead into a world of dark choices and hidden dangers. Intellectual brilliance unfettered from any spiritual mooring operates in a narrow spectrum of light. What is needed to guide us through these perilous times is the illuminating light of spiritual insight.

In this regard, a story from the Brihadaranyaka Upanishad is instructive:

Master: How do you see when the sun goes down?
Pupil: In that case, I see by the moonlight.
Master: How do you see when the moon is no longer present?
Pupil: When the moon is no longer present, by candlelight.
Master: And then when you blow out the candle and there is no sun, then no moon, and then no candle, how do you see then?
Pupil: Well, Master, somehow I see by the light within.[5]

The Mystery of the "Ring-Pass-Not"

One of the intriguing occult terms found in H. P. Blavatsky's *The Secret Doctrine* is what is called the "Ring-Pass-Not" (1:129). It is prefaced by a series of geometrical symbols, which can be interpreted numerically as representing the mathematical value *pi*, a number—3.1415—used to calculate the circumference of a given circle when only the diameter of that circle is known. In his *Occult Glossary*, G. de Purucker only deepens the mystery when he provides this definition of the Ring-Pass-Not:

> A profoundly mystical and suggestive term signifying the circle or bounds of frontiers within which is contained the consciousness of those who are still under the sway of the delusion of separateness—and this applies whether the Ring be large or small. It does not signify any one especial occasion or condition, but is a general term applicable to any state in which an entity, having reached a certain stage of evolutionary growth of the unfolding of consciousness, finds itself unable to pass into a still higher state because of some delusion under which the consciousness is laboring, be that delusion mental or spiritual.[6]

De Purucker goes on to explain that, although the phenomenon of a Ring-Pass-Not applies to globes, planetary chains, solar systems, and so forth, the main point to remember is that it pertains in some mysterious way to "phases or states of consciousness." Blavatsky adds to the mystery when she says, "The full Initiate *knows* that the Ring 'Pass-Not' is neither a locality nor can it be measured by distance, but that it exists in the absoluteness of infinity" (1:131).

As a further illustration of how the Ring-Pass-Not relates to fields of consciousness in living entities, de Purucker suggests that for animals, it concerns their inability to exercise the power of reflective self-consciousness—an ability which is distinctly human. We can only speculate what it may represent in relation to the field of human consciousness.

Is Theosophy Too Abstract?

One of the common complaints of those encountering Theosophy for the first time is that our literature is too abstract. "Of what practical use is it? How is it relevant to my life?" Because these questions have merit, Theosophical journals often feature articles explaining the application of Theosophical principles to daily life. Yet there is something to be said in defense of the abstract nature of much of our literature. Reading abstruse passages from *The Secret Doctrine*, for example, challenges our mental faculties in ways to which we may be unaccustomed. That part of our mind that deals with empirical data is quite different from the part that comprehends universal principles, and both aspects are necessary.

Modern science uses the inductive method of investigation, but Madame Blavatsky reminds us that, for Initiates,[7] the deductive method was the preferred mode of inquiry:

> It must be remembered that the study of Occultism proceeds from Universals to Particulars, and not the reverse, as accepted by Science. As Plato was an Initiate, he very naturally used the former method, while Aristotle, never having been initiated, scoffed at his master, and, elaborating a system of his own, left it as an heirloom to be adopted and improved by [Francis] Bacon.[8]

Whereas the Initiates concerned themselves with a few universal truths, the modern scientist deals with a plethora of facts in the hope of arriving at truth. In his book *Man, God and the Universe*, I. K. Taimni argues that it is easier to deal with a few abstract principles than with an endless stream of facts and data:

> Once we have derived or discovered a principle by correct and reliable methods we can depend upon it under all kinds of circumstances. But when we are dealing with a mass of detailed facts we are liable to trip any moment. The reason for this is obvious. All principles and relations exist in the realm of the Universal Mind as eternal verities and are not subject to change or modification. The phenomena, on the other hand, form a flowing stream every part of which is changing all the time.[9]

Because of the ephemeral nature of the phenomenal world, methods of practical application need to be modified as circumstances change. Nothing in this world remains the same, even for an instant. As sailors of old set their gaze on the polestar above in order to navigate the restless ocean below, students of the Ageless Wisdom fix their sights on the eternal verities as they traverse the ever-changing and sometimes tumultuous sea of life. What can be more practical than that?

Untimely Departures

Why is it that some great souls die so young, their all-too-brief appearance on the world stage resembling shooting stars, flashing momentarily against the dark abyss? John Keats died in his twenty-fifth year, but not before leaving behind a legacy that later established him as one of the leading poets of the English Romantic era; his "Ode on a Grecian Urn" remains popular to this day. Percy Bysshe Shelley, a contemporary of Keats, died at the age of twenty-nine; he authored *Prometheus Unbound* and is said to be one of the finest lyric poets of his time. Emily Brontë had time for only one novel before she died at age thirty, but her *Wuthering Heights* has had numerous film adaptations, from as early as 1920 to as recently as 2011. The Austrian composer Franz Schubert managed to write ten symphonies, eleven string quartets, and assorted chamber music before he died at thirty-one. And if anybody ever deserved the label of *genius*, it was Amadeus Mozart, whose musical oeuvre was astonishing, covering virtually every genre of his day. He never saw his thirty-sixth birthday. The Dutch painter Johannes Vermeer passed away at forty-three, his output consisting of mostly domestic scenes; more than three hundred years after his death, one of Vermeer's oil paintings inspired the movie *Girl with a Pearl Earring*, starring Colin Firth.

That the sojourn in this world of these extraordinary people ended much too soon is apparent to the aesthetic sensibility. A thoughtful person cannot help but wonder whether their early demise was due to *chance* or to *design*. If the capricious hand of fate was at work, these early deaths may be considered to be nothing more than items on the list of life's tragedies. But what if these truncated lives were preordained, so to speak? What if they were meant to be?

In Mahatma Letter 68, oblique references are made to the idea that the soul comes into an incarnation "destined to live" a certain span of time, an idea that seems compatible with the idea that each incarnation has a purpose.[10] Could it be that the life of a Mozart or a Keats was intended to grace the stage of life not for more than a few years but just enough for them to bestow their sublime gifts to humanity? We can only speculate. If the early departure of such souls was one of chance, we see tragedy. But if a hidden purpose was at work, the meaning of which we are unable to divine, we behold a mystery. Fortunately, the fruit of their creativity remains, enriching our lives and uplifting our spirits.

Chapter 8

THE THEOSOPHICAL SOCIETY

Teaching with Humility

When we are moved by a profound idea that seemingly provides the key to unlocking some of life's mysteries, it is natural to want others to embrace that idea, too. When we experience an epiphany into the nature of the human condition, we may feel a powerful urge to "share" our insight with others. In this heightened state of zeal, we may even frame our new-found fervor in the words of the Gospel: "Ye are the light of the world . . . let your light so shine before men" (Matt. 5:14, 16). But before we embark on a campaign to save the world, it may be wise to temper our momentary zeal by recalling the words of an old English proverb: Discretion is the better part of valor.

The tendency to impose our particular views on others is not something exclusive to any one culture or people but is a universal trait, one that has been on display throughout human history. Sometimes it may surface in Theosophical gatherings. The late Shirley Nicholson addressed this potential problem: "One of the most precious benefits of the Theosophical Society is the freedom of thought it offers. This may be one of the most important reasons that the Society has survived and remained viable for over one hundred years."[1]

Because of this long-standing policy of tolerance toward the views of others, the Theosophical Society is distinctly different from many other religious and esoteric organizations, which often require their members or followers to accept a certain set of beliefs or views.

To suggest that Theosophists strive to be open minded does not preclude the fact that many of us have strong opinions, often becoming passionate and animated when discussing esoteric ideas. This is not a bad thing as long as we retain a sense of humility, recognizing that our present level of understanding is quite finite, our level of ignorance nearly infinite.

At one time, we may not have been receptive to the ideas that now provide great meaning in our lives. The power of comprehension grows with time. Yesterday we may not have possessed the wisdom we have today, and tomorrow our current store of "wisdom" may appear somewhat limited, as we continue to expand our intellectual horizons. There is also the matter of interpretation. Just as music conductors may bring different interpretations to the symphonies of Beethoven or Mozart, students of Theosophy may bring various interpretations to the timeless principles of Theosophy. When teaching Theosophy, therefore, we will find it more effective to use a "soft touch" rather than to adopt an unyielding and authoritative approach. New ideas presented too forcefully often create resistance or rejection among the intended audience, whereas an impartial and reasonable presentation is more likely to gain a fair hearing.

The Importance of History

It has been said that a nation that does not respect its own history will have no future worthy of respect. If you don't know where you've been, how can you know where you're going? Perhaps the same idea holds true for organizations and institutions. Take the Theosophical Society, for example, a worldwide organization found in over seventy countries around the world, carrying on its mission since its founding in 1875. Although people become members for a variety of reasons, gaining knowledge of the organization's history may not be one of them. Yet an understanding of the Society's distinct and colorful past imparts a deep sense of appreciation and shapes one's perspective on its true mission in the world.

To the extent that some members of the Theosophical Society are ignorant of its history, we have a situation that is merely symptomatic of a larger societal issue. For as recently as September 2007, the Intercollegiate Studies Institute reported that fewer than 50 percent of the college seniors polled in the United States could identify the phrase, "We hold these truths to be self-evident, that all men are created equal," as being a line from the Declaration of Independence. This level of civic ignorance is troubling, to say the least. But such a myopic view of the world is not limited to students in this country. The *Australian* reported in November 2007 that a majority of high-school sophomores didn't know the British queen was their head of state. And a 2007 poll conducted in Sweden showed that 90 percent of the students had no clue what the Gulag was. Think about it. Tens of millions of people perished in the communist Gulags during the Cold War, enduring unspeakable hardships before expiring, and such a glaring fact of history doesn't even register as a blip on the radar screen of today's hip, plugged-in, high-tech youngsters, who are perhaps more fluent in citing the names of contestants that have participated in the popular *American Idol* TV show.

In her well-documented book, *A Short History of the Theosophical Society*, Josephine Ransom suggests that when we study the Society's history, we should "watch the steady fulfillment of a purpose no matter what the obstacles. That purpose burns, an unquenchable beacon, along the pathway of the Society. It is unquenchable because its flame is fed from sources which we do not supply, and which none may extinguish save those who in their wisdom lit it so long ago."[2]

White Lotus Day

Throughout the Theosophical world, May 8 is known as White Lotus Day, a day set aside to commemorate the passing of Helena Petrovna Blavatsky, the founder of the Theosophical Society. More than any other person, she was responsible for resurrecting the forgotten truths of the wisdom tradition and bringing them into the modern era. But it was no cakewalk, for she accomplished this in the face of relentless opposition and caustic ridicule. For this, all of us whose lives have been touched deeply by Theosophy owe her a great debt of gratitude. Without her fiery courage and unending self-sacrifice, how much poorer our lives would be.

In this passage from the preface of *The Secret Doctrine*, where HPB refers to herself in the third person, she strikes a tone of unshakable confidence: "Abuse she is accustomed to; calumny she is daily acquainted with; at slander she smiles in silent contempt" (1:viii). In another marvelous passage, she dismisses her critics with splendid disdain: "To my judges, past and future, therefore—whether they are serious literary critics, or those howling dervishes in literature who judge a book according to the popularity or unpopularity of the author's name, who, hardly glancing at its contents, fasten like lethal *bacilli* on the weakest points of the body—I have nothing to say" (ibid.).

Can there be any doubt about the skill she had with words? The poet Robert Frost once said, "The right reader of a good poem can tell the moment it strikes him that he has taken an immortal wound—that he will never get over it."[3] Similarly, HPB had the rare ability to strike people in that fashion. Many of us freely admit that we, too, have been "wounded" by her writings and, moreover, we are not in a hurry to get over it.

The Remarkable Healing Powers
of Colonel Henry Steel Olcott

Colonel Henry Steel Olcott was the cofounder and first president of the Theosophical Society. Theosophical historians remember him for his capable administrative and executive abilities. During the Society's formative years, his organizational skills proved to be invaluable. But there was another, more mysterious side to Colonel Olcott that is sometimes overlooked. In addition to his executive skills, he possessed an amazing ability to heal the sick and did so on numerous occasions.

The second volume of Olcott's *Old Diary Leaves* describes a number of such instances, which took place in 1882–83. Olcott had been familiar with the phenomenon of mesmeric healing for over thirty years but had never done more than dabble in it. While traveling in Ceylon (now Sri Lanka) during August 1882, he began exercising his latent power of healing with astonishing results. After having had some initial success curing dozens of patients with limb paralysis, he noted, "With the rapid growth of confidence in myself, my magnetic power multiplied itself enormously, and what I had needed days to accomplish with a patient, at the commencement, could now be done within a half hour."[4]

Being a matter-of-fact person, Colonel Olcott also described the nuisance factor that accompanied these miraculous healings: "Within a week or so my house was besieged by sick persons from dawn until late at night, all clamoring for the laying on of my hands. They grew so importunate at last that I was at my wit's end how to dispose of them. . . . They would besiege me in my bedroom before I was dressed, dog my every step, give me no time for meals, and keep pressing me, no matter how tired and exhausted I might be."[5]

Henry Steel Olcott was a man who could take minor inconveniences in stride without losing his greater sense of purpose. He demonstrated this over and over again, and we could all take a lesson from him in this regard. Throughout his many years of service to the Theosophical Society, his one overriding motivation was to serve the Masters of Wisdom and, through them, humanity.

Doctrine without Dogma

From time to time, members of the Theosophical Society need to be reminded that although the Society has no dogma, it does not follow that it has no doctrines. More to the point, it is the body of teachings known as the Ageless Wisdom, or Theosophy, which has a number of cardinal principles often referred to as "doctrines." In some circles, doctrine becomes crystallized into dogma and is then generally accepted without question. This is unfortunate, since a dogmatic attitude tends to discourage free and open-minded inquiry. It occurs in organizations ranging from religious institutions to military academies, from political organizations to organized labor. A distinguishing feature of the Theosophical Society, however, is that its members are free to form their own understanding of Theosophical teachings. They are encouraged to study, ask questions, and interpret, because Theosophy is not a creed to be accepted as an article of faith.

Yet, despite this approach, which the Society has taken since its inception, the very word *doctrine* seems to make some people uncomfortable and even a bit feisty. For example, Richard Ihle, a frequent contributor to *The American Theosophist*, dismisses the whole idea of doctrine without dogma as a "somewhat oxymoronic opinion."[6] Others take a different view.

Shirley Nicholson, author of *Ancient Wisdom—Modern Insight*, stated, "It is obvious then that there is a coherent body of teachings in Theosophy, a doctrine which can be studied."[7] World traveler and Theosophical lecturer Joy Mills was in agreement: "It is scarcely possible to deny the existence of such a doctrine in a society that calls itself *Theosophical*."[8] She cited the Theosophical Worldview as an example of a well-crafted statement of Theosophical doctrine.

This argument is not to suggest that there is no room for creative inquiry. "Obviously, there can be an endless number of ways to interpret and apply Theosophical principles," observed Theosophical scholar Emily Sellon.[9] There is no limit as to how one may choose to explore key ideas such as unity, polarity, involution, evolution, cycles, reincarnation, and Karma.

Statements of Theosophical doctrine are offered, therefore, not to establish a rigid orthodoxy of verbal formulations, but to assist the open-minded inquirer in discovering the reality of eternal and living truths.

The Practicality of Ideas

Every now and then it's necessary to go back to basics. For example, a baseball player mired in a hitting slump may be advised by the coach to modify his stance in the batter's box; in football, a defensive lineman may occasionally find he needs to improve his blocking technique; a political party may be compelled to revisit its guiding principles after a stinging defeat at the ballot box; even a virtuoso violinist may sometimes practice long tones while checking for proper intonation. Similarly, members of the Theosophical Society benefit by periodical reflection on the Society's purpose and mission in the world. The notable Theosophist G. de Purucker, circa 1940, had this to say:

The Theosophist is often asked what practical good the Theosophical Society is doing in and for the world, and the answer is
simple enough and direct to the point of the question. We work
with ideas, and we try to show men that there is nothing more
practical . . . and more forceful than an idea. Ideas shake civilizations and over-throw them. Look what has happened in the past.
What brought such changes about? Ideas. . . .

Show me something more practical than an idea. If ideas over-
throw civilizations, they also build them up. The whole work of
the Theosophical Society is to fill the minds and hearts of men
with ideals of grandeur, inspiring them to ever nobler, more un-
selfish, and [more] altruistic objectives; to give men and women
thoughts that they can live and die by. Show me something more
practical than this. This is our main work.[10]

Dr. de Purucker was a deep student of *The Secret Doctrine* and
the author of several outstanding books on Theosophy. Although
he wrote these words nearly eighty years ago, his message is just as
vital and relevant today as it was then.

Diversity, not Orthodoxy

For students of Theosophy, familiarity with its doctrines is desirable—a doctrinaire approach to their study is not. These doctrines,
or principles, have been enunciated differently by various commentators, each of whom may have some unique insight or perspective.
The timeless truths of Theosophy are such that no one writer or
person can claim to have the final word. As Montaigne said, "Truth
and reason are common to everyone, and no more belong to the
man who first spoke them than to the man who says them later."[11]

In Theosophical circles it is often noted that none of us are
experts, that we are all students. That seems to be a very healthy
point of view, for it helps prevent our intellectual inquiry from

devolving from one that is fresh and open minded to one that is rigid and predictable. Cicero once observed: "The authority of those who want to teach is often an obstacle to those who want to learn."[12] Having said this, it is generally recognized that some students have been at it longer than others and therefore possess a considerable storehouse of knowledge and wisdom. That is a very different thing from posing as an authority. And while it is quite legitimate that we acknowledge authorities in the fields of medicine, engineering, jurisprudence, and other areas of secular knowledge, it is quite improper—even absurd—to assume the mantle of "authority" in the field of Theosophical inquiry.

Those who are widely read are likely to have a broader perspective than those who are not. These words from T. S. Eliot, though made in a different context, are relevant to our point:

> Wide reading is not valuable as a kind of hoarding, an accumulation of knowledge, or what sometimes is meant by the term "a well-stocked mind." It is valuable because in the process of being affected by one powerful personality after another, we cease to be dominated by any one, or by any small number.[13]

I think Eliot is making a very salient point. When we expose ourselves to different points of view, we are not as likely to allow our opinions to crystalize into a rigid certainty, something that may occur when we become overly enamored with the thoughts of a single but influential writer. And consider these words of H. P. Blavatsky:

> Orthodoxy in Theosophy is a thing neither possible nor desirable. It is diversity of opinion, within certain limits, that keeps the Theosophical Society a living and healthy body. . . . Were it not . . . such healthy divergences would be impossible, and the Society would degenerate into a sect, in which a narrow and stereotyped creed would take the place of the living and breathing spirit of Truth and an ever-growing Knowledge.[14]

As a farmer's soil is enriched when crops are rotated yearly, so, too, will our understanding of Theosophy be enriched if we expose our minds to diverse and varied thought.

Freedom of Thought

A fine line is crossed when we begin by trying to help someone and end up trying to control them. What starts as an act of kindness ends up as an imposition of will. Since this is not an uncommon human failing, members of the Theosophical Society are reminded that we should respect a person's freedom to think and make their own choices.

In 1924, the General Council of the Theosophical Society adopted the Freedom of Thought Resolution, which states: "No teacher, or writer, from H. P. Blavatsky downwards, has any authority to impose his teachings or opinions on members." Commenting in the 1987 fall issue of *The American Theosophist*, then President Dorothy Abbenhouse noted: "Members of the Society are free to think, to believe, to work for any truth they find valid; at the same time each must respect the freedom of all other members to find their own truths."

With human nature being what it is, this approach goes against the grain for some people. But while sharing Theosophical ideas is one thing, imposing those ideas on others is something else. For instance, one might think: *Theosophy has made a great difference in my life. Therefore, I want to make you a beneficiary of my infallible wisdom.* That may be a bit of an overstatement, but perhaps not by much.

The New York literary critic Lionel Trilling once said, "Some paradox of our nature leads us, when once we have made our fellow men the objects of our enlightened interest, to go on to make them the objects of our pity, then of our wisdom, ultimately of our coercion."[15] It is indeed a slippery slope when a desire to alleviate suffering ends up causing misery on an even greater scale.

Remembering White Lotus Day

Can you identify the nineteenth-century author who wrote these words? Here's a hint: the author was not a man.

> Such is the heart of many a woman. The first gracious word, the first affectionate caress, falling on her aching heart, takes root there deeply.

Was it Jane Austen? Charlotte Brontë? Elizabeth Browning? None of the above. Instead, this romantic passage is from a little-known story called "Legend of the Night Flower" and was penned by the same author that brought you *Isis Unveiled*, *The Secret Doctrine*, and *The Voice of the Silence*.[16] So why mention this obscure work? Simply to illustrate the varied literary skill of the Theosophical Society's founder, H. P. Blavatsky.

Madame Blavatsky passed away on May 8, 1891. Since then, Theosophists around the world celebrate May 8 as WHITE LOTUS DAY in order to commemorate the life and work of our beloved founder. Anybody who has been moved and inspired by her writings owes her a debt of gratitude. One of her teachers once made a wonderfully self-deprecating statement: "Ingratitude is not among our vices."[17] Shall it then be one of ours?

Despite her human failings, how can our hearts not go out to the heroic warrior whom Geoffrey Barborka affectionately referred to as the "light-bringer"?[18] HPB endured much physical and mental suffering for the cause of Theosophy, while "ever and ever bringing secrets forth." She was subjected to a torrent of ridicule, slander, and withering invective, but she courageously battled the forces of Darkness to bring us the Light. For all that she withstood and accomplished, the heart responds with undying gratitude and love. Such is the heart of a true Theosophist.

Chapter 9

THE THREE OBJECTS OF THE THEOSOPHICAL SOCIETY

The First Object

To form a nucleus of the universal brotherhood of humanity,
without distinction of race, creed, sex, caste, or color . . .

How easy it is to pay lip service to the first Object of the Theosophical Society! Who doesn't embrace the idea of living in peace and harmony with others? There is no great risk attached to holding such a view in today's ever-shrinking world where people increasingly recognize the necessity for concord in the global community. But while embracing the idea of universal goodwill is easy, putting it into practice may not be so simple.

The Theosophical writer Ernest Wood gave voice to this apparent truth: "It is easy to go and live in a forest, and from that seclusion feel good will toward all mankind; but it is another matter if you have to take your part in the struggle of life."[1] Yes, indeed. How easy it is to feel harmonious when surrounded by the warmth of friends and like-minded colleagues. How easy it is to feel serene when in the company of those who share our views and opinions. But notice how quickly our sense of brotherhood turns to discord when we are obliged to endure the company of an unpleasant and disagreeable person. How quickly our sense of tranquility gives way to resentment and frustration when Karma forces us to endure an apparent injustice. We may even identify with Linus, a character from the "Peanuts" comic strip, who once professed, "I love humanity; it's people I can't stand."

The time when the spiritual seeker could retire to the secluded life of the ashram, temple, or monastery is largely a thing of the past. Very few people can afford to take that approach today. Those who are serious about developing a rich, inner life of the spirit must attempt to do so while living amidst the chaotic turmoil of the outer world.

In her writings, H. P. Blavatsky repeatedly emphasized the importance of brotherhood as a guiding principle: "It is only by all men becoming brothers and all women sisters, and by all practicing in their daily lives true brotherhood and true sisterhood, that the real human solidarity . . . can ever be attained."[2] No matter how learned or erudite we may become in the metaphysics of Theosophy, let us not forget that the true measure of a Theosophist lies not in a proud and self-centered intellect but in an open and loving heart.

The Second Object

To encourage the comparative study of
religion, philosophy, and science . . .

On one level, the intent of the second Object of the Theosophical Society seems obvious: to encourage people to acquire a general familiarity with the world's major religious traditions, the key ideas from Western and Eastern schools of philosophy, and the latest theories and trends in modern science. Since its inception in 1875, the Theosophical Society has played a major role in fostering an attitude of understanding and goodwill between people of different faiths. It has been instrumental in bringing the wisdom tradition of the East to a Western audience, as well as rediscovering some of the Western esoteric traditions that had been ignored or forgotten over the centuries. In the field of science, H. P. Blavatsky railed against the materialistic attitudes held by scientists of her day, but as a new generation of thinkers began to emerge in the twentieth century, leading scientists such as David Bohm, Albert Einstein, and Werner Heisenberg put forth theories that seemed very compatible with those found in *The Secret Doctrine.*

On another level, the intent of the second Object may be less obvious. When the founders of the Society framed the second Object, they had in mind another purpose beyond the mere broadening of one's intellectual horizons, which was to encourage the type of study aimed at discovering universal and underlying truths. Comparative study was meant not to be an end in itself but rather the means to uncover fundamental and eternal verities. We can continue accumulating more surface knowledge for the rest of our days, but to what end? Every underlying principle can be expressed in a multitude of ways; therefore, our search for knowledge will never exhaust the finite expressions of the Infinite.

Once we understand the basic principle behind the phenomena, all else falls into place; but if we get lost in the terminology of various disciplines we end up confused and bewildered.

To put it another way, one of the benefits of reading in this manner is that it enables the student to distinguish the outer expressions from the inner realities that those expressions are meant to symbolize. As the motto of the Theosophical Society states, "There is no religion higher than Truth."

The Role of Study in the Theosophical Life

Annie Besant once said that the foundation for a truly Theosophical life rests upon the three pillars of study, meditation, and service.

Let's consider what it means to study. For many people, study implies reading, gaining new information and ideas, comparing that to what we already know, and then storing it on our internal hard drive. Dr. Besant, however, had something quite different in mind when she emphasized the role of study. For instance, we can make a lifetime practice of reading articles and books while nothing fundamental changes within us. We remain essentially the same person, week after week, year after year, until we cry out in anguish like Goethe's Faust:

> I have pursued, alas, philosophy,
> Jurisprudence, and medicine,
> And, help me God, theology,
> With fervent zeal through thick and thin.
> And here, poor fool, I stand once more,
> No wiser than I was before.[3]

Let's consider the second Object of the Theosophical Society: "To encourage the comparative study of religion, philosophy, and science." We might ask, comparative study to what end? Why this emphasis on study? Surely, academic achievement is not the *raison d'être* of the second Object.

In his *Introductory Studies in Theosophy*, Adelaide Gardner gives us a clue:

> The comparative method of study necessitates the use of the higher or subtler element in the mind. The higher mind is synthetic and unifying, as compared with the contentiousness of the analytical mind, used for ordinary objective thinking, which is separative in its action.[4]

I think Annie Besant would agree that one purpose of the second Object is to activate the higher faculties of mind, thereby enabling the seeker to go beyond the domain of empirical knowledge into the realm of unitary wisdom, wherein shines the unfading light of truth. Endless study leading only to the accumulation of more knowledge has limited value in the spiritual life, but the type of study that facilitates a state of interior wisdom has been praised by the greatest of philosophers throughout the ages.

The Third Object

*To investigate unexplained laws of nature
and the powers latent in humanity . . .*

The wording of the Theosophical Society's three Objects was revised a number of times during the early years of the Society, but they have remained essentially unchanged since 1896.[5] Many of our members associate the third Object primarily with psychic powers such as clairvoyance, clairaudience, precognition, telepathy, and the like. Certainly, the scope of the third Object includes these types of interesting phenomena, but it really goes much deeper than that. Seventy-eight years after the founding of the Society, the Rohit Mehta observed, "We have yet to understand the full significance of the third Object."[6] Oddly enough, this may still be the case today.

Over the years, serious students of Theosophy have given us hints as to the inner meaning of the third Object. In *Human Regeneration*, Radha Burnier suggests that "we must see the connection between the three Objects . . . to the unfoldment of the human consciousness."[7] Joy Mills has suggested that the third Object relates to both "a way of knowing" and "a way of living."[8] By *knowing* she meant not an accumulation of intellectual data but rather a "process of inner comprehension." Hugh Shearman offered another insight: "Occult truths are never hidden from us by anybody. We reveal or conceal them ourselves individually by what we are and what we are not yet."[9]

In other words, the methods used to gain ordinary knowledge are not sufficient to comprehend the hidden laws of nature and unfold the latent powers within.

If we are unhappy and frustrated with life, the possession of psychic powers will not bring us the inner peace we so desperately seek. At best, they provide a temporary diversion; at worst, they can lead to psychological instability and impairment of physical health. Serious students of Theosophy agree that we must first change ourselves before we can safely acquire intimate knowledge of nature's occult forces. This is why it has long been said, "Live the life if you are to come to the wisdom."

Psychic Development

An exploration of the Theosophical Society's third Object, "to investigate unexplained laws of nature and the powers latent in humanity," includes the study of psychic research conducted by investigators in this field. Very few individuals have the natural abilities or trained psychic faculties necessary to do the kind of direct clairvoyant investigation conducted by now-deceased Society members such as Dora Kunz, Phoebe Bendit, Geoffrey Hodson, and Charles Leadbeater. In fact, it is inadvisable for people to develop those faculties without having first met certain moral and ethical qualifications such as those listed in the spiritual guidebook *At the Feet of the Master*. The reader of that book is given this cautionary advice: "Have no desire for psychic powers . . . to force them too soon often brings in its train much trouble."[10]

A serious exploration of the third Object, however, need not involve the use of clairvoyance. Writing on the subject, Joy Mills has suggested, "We are not just talking about investigating or acquiring a certain knowledge or understanding of universal processes, but of coming, through a developing intuition, to a direct perception of those universals in terms of their reflections in [our] own inherent capacities, our own immortal and deific powers."[11] In other words, while the spiritual neophyte is given numerous warnings against the premature development of psychic powers, the same warnings do not seem to apply to the development of spiritual intuition.

Still, there are those who succumb to the glamour associated with psychic powers despite repeated warnings. Perhaps one stark example (and there are many) may serve to illustrate my point. A couple of years ago I received a desperate letter from a prisoner who had dabbled with psychic development. He had fallen into a month-long depression following the death of a close friend. "I began to build my own world in my mind, characters and all. At the end of the forty or so days, I started to hear the voice of one of the characters I created in my head. It started off faint, and then became more audible." He then began to hear other voices. "When they first arrived, they were at a peaceful level; but as time has progressed they have become malicious, angry, and lustful. The situation is getting a bit intense."

If we attempt to force psychic development before we are ready, we may be opening doors that are better left closed—at least for the time being. Invisible forces surround us: some are benevolent, some are benign, and others may be malignant. It is well to re-member that once we have opened the doorway to the unseen worlds, it may be difficult or impossible to close that door again.

Latent Powers

In his 1875 Inaugural Address to the Theosophical Society, President Henry S. Olcott declared: "We should make ourselves familiar with the manifold powers of the human soul and test the claims for the potency of the human will."[12] Also, "Every human being contains within himself vast potentialities," said one of the Adepts.[13]

This brings us again to the third Object of the Theosophical Society, which encourages members "to investigate unexplained laws of nature and the powers latent in humanity." Whereas the Theosophist can approach the second Object (the comparative study of religion, philosophy, and science) largely through selected readings and thoughtful reflection, the scope of the third Object suggests a somewhat circumscribed role for books, journals, and other written material. A different approach is implied.

It has been suggested that we adopt an attitude of open-minded inquiry. As Olcott further stated in his inaugural address, "We seek, inquire, reject nothing without cause, accept nothing without proof: we are students, not teachers." That statement also describes the attitude of the true scientist who generally tests his or her theories under controlled laboratory conditions with empirical methods. A meaningful exploration of the third Object likewise requires the student to test various occult theories. There is a huge difference, however, between the methods employed by the scientist and those used by the student of occult laws and phenomena. In the latter case, the methods are largely subjective and, more importantly, the student *becomes* the laboratory.

An exploration of the third Object is an undertaking not without its share of perils and pitfalls. Idle curiosity is not a sufficient motive for probing the powers that lie dormant within the human soul. The careful student will find many helpful hints and suggestions in the vast literature of the Theosophical Society.

Chapter 10

PROLOGUES TO
THE VOICE OF THE SILENCE

A Spiritual Guidebook

H. P. Blavatsky was a prolific writer whose *Collected Writings* alone span fourteen volumes. Yet she is better known for her two monumental works, *Isis Unveiled* and *The Secret Doctrine,* published in 1877 and 1888 respectively, and which together contain nearly three thousand pages. *Isis* created quite a sensation with its remarkable but sprawling, panoramic view of the wisdom tradition. The work for which she is best known today, *The Secret Doctrine*, presents a daring depiction of the origin and essential nature of humanity and the universe. After producing a work of epic proportions, many writers understandably would have taken some time off to recuperate, but not Blavatsky. In 1889, one year later and two years before her death, she wrote two smaller but still important books: *The Key to Theosophy* and *The Voice of the Silence.* The first was an instructional book, while the second was a spiritual guidebook containing a little over three hundred verses. It is the latter work that this prologue, and the other prolegomena to follow, will address.

First, a brief comparison of the *Voice* to the other three works mentioned may be helpful. For instance, the style of *Isis* might be described as discursive; so much so, in fact, that the reader may easily lose track of the overarching theme while trekking through the labyrinth of digressions, citations, and topical commentary. Although the *Secret Doctrine* puts forth the fundamental doctrines of the wisdom tradition in magnificent fashion, it is not a book of instruction. John Algeo has described it as a "heuristic" book, which is to say, a book of discovery.[1] It is *The Key to Theosophy* that holds the distinction of being the only instructional book ever penned by Blavatsky. It is written in the expository style typical of such books but framed in a question-answer format, with HPB filling both roles.

The very first verse of the *Voice* might lead the reader to believe it also to be a book of instruction, beginning as it does with the words, "These instructions are for. . . ." But he would be wrong. Although the *Voice* contains teachings put forth as precepts, it is essentially a book whose purpose is to inspire rather than instruct; its message is directed at the heart, not the intellect. It was intended to serve as a spiritual guidebook for those who desire to tread the path of altruism in the service of humanity. The fact that it is still being published and read 125 years after its initial publication suggests that it has enduring value and will continue to be a source of inspiration and guidance for many generations to come.

"The Grandest Thing"

The Voice of the Silence was written during the summer of 1889 while Mme. Blavatsky was staying with friends in Fontainebleau, France. By all accounts, it was written quickly and followed on the heels of *The Key to Theosophy,* which was written earlier that same year. The first book review for the *Voice* appeared in the February 1890 issue of *The Theosophist;* the reviewer whimsically compared *Light on the Path*, a mystical treatise written by Mabel Collins four years earlier, to the newly published *Voice of the Silence*:

The difference between these two works will strike some people as like that between a magnificent melody by Verdi and a fragment of Wagner;—a simile which the admirers respectively of melody and of harmony (with a trifle of discord thrown in) will each take as a compliment to their taste.[2]

One of the friends who was with Mme. Blavatsky in Fontainebleau was Annie Besant. In an 1895 lecture, Besant recalled the fascinating spectacle of watching Blavatsky as she labored over her manuscript:

She wrote it at Fontainebleau, and the greater part was done when I was with her, and I sat in the room while she was writing it. I know that she did not write it referring to any books, but she wrote it down steadily, hour after hour, exactly as though she were writing either from memory or from reading it where no book was. She produced, in the evening, that manuscript that I saw her write as I sat with her, and asked myself and others to correct it for English, for she said that she had written it so quickly that it was sure to be bad. We did not alter in that more than a few words, and it remains as a specimen of marvelously beautiful literary work.[3]

Olcott gives a similar account in *Old Diary Leaves*, in which he describes Blavatsky during the writing of *Isis Unveiled*:

To watch her at work was a rare and never-to-be-forgotten experience. We usually sat at opposite sides of one big table, and I could see her every movement. Her pen would be flying over the page, when she would suddenly stop, look out into space with the vacant eye of the clairvoyant seer, shorten her vision as though to look at something held invisibly in the air before her, and begin copying on her paper what she saw. The quotation finished, her eyes would resume their natural expression and she would go on writing until again stopped by a similar interruption.[4]

As fascinating as all that may be, none of it would matter one whit if *The Voice* had not been of the caliber to cause the Gnostic scholar G. R. S. Mead to characterize it as "the grandest thing in all our Theosophical literature."[5]

Ninety, Thirty-Nine, and Three

The Voice of the Silence is a remarkable book in more ways than one. As is the case with *Isis Unveiled* and *The Secret Doctrine*, eyewitness accounts of how it was written is a story in itself, further adding to the mystery surrounding H. P. Blavatsky. Those who are intrigued by such mysteries would profit from reading C. W. Leadbeater's preface to *Talks on the Path of Occultism,* volume 2, where he speculates about what mysterious methods Blavatsky may have used in writing the *Voice.*

On a more pellucid level, the *Voice* holds other points of interest. Structurally, it is comprised of three parts. What first strikes the observant reader is the odd term used to designate those parts; not only is it unusual, but when the rationale behind its use is understood, further questions arise. Authors most commonly divide their works into *chapters*; indeed, Blavatsky did that in *Isis Unveiled.* Sometimes a book is divided into *sections*, as is *The Key to Theosophy.* Still others, particularly longer works, are apportioned into "books," as in Plato's *Republic*, Montaigne's *Essays,* St. Augustine's *Confessions,* and Milton's *Paradise Lost.* Why, then, did Blavatsky use the peculiar term *fragments* when organizing the contents of *The Voice of the Silence?*

To understand why, the reader must first realize that it is a translation. Blavatsky was not its *author* but its *translator.* She makes this clear in the first sentence of her preface: "The following pages are derived from *The Book of Golden Precepts.* . . ." According to her, it contained some ninety short treatises, and of those she memorized thirty-nine, only three of which comprise *The Voice of the Silence.* When and where did Blavatsky come into contact with

The Book of Golden Precepts? Most likely, it was some thirty years prior to the publication of the *Voice,* when Blavatsky spent three years in Nepal (some scholars say Tibet). If that is true, the choice of the term *fragments* is apropos, since the three fragments of the *Voice* are small parts, or fragments, of a much larger work.

The reader may then ask, why translate only three? Why not translate all ninety treatises? In her preface to the *Voice,* Blavatsky explains that they could not be "given to a world too selfish and too much attached to the objects of sense to be in any way prepared to receive such exalted ethics in the right spirit." That answer may not satisfy the cynics or skeptics, but if they would consider to what extent the sublime ethics given to the world two thousand years ago in the Sermon on the Mount have been put into practice today, Blavatsky's answer seems eminently plausible.

To the Few

How many readers pay attention to the dedication page of a book? Other than for the spouse or immediate family of the author to whom they are often directed, dedication pages usually don't warrant much attention. But this is not the case with the major works of Blavatsky. The inscription in *Isis Unveiled* states: "The Author dedicates these volumes to the Theosophical Society which was founded at New York, AD 1875, to study the subjects on which they treat." *The Secret Doctrine* has this dedication: "This Work I dedicate to all True Theosophists in every Country, and of every Race, for they called it forth, and for them it was recorded." And the dedication from *The Key to Theosophy* reads: "Dedicated by 'H.P.B.' to all her Pupils, that They may Learn and Teach in their turn."

Each of these dedications reveals something about the book and its target audience. If we understand the word *pupil* to include not only those who had the good fortune of studying directly with

Blavatsky but also those later generations of Theosophists who had yet to be born, the potential audience addressed is fairly large.

But we encounter something very different with *The Voice of the Silence,* whose inscription is as simple as it is curious: "Dedicated to the few."

Obviously, HPB did not write the *Voice* for a mass audience, but why dedicate it to "the few"? Why not the Theosophical Society? Why not all genuine Theosophists? Or, at the very least, why not dedicate it to her pupils?

The answer becomes apparent in the third verse of the first fragment: "Having become indifferent to objects of perception, the pupil must seek out the Rājā of the senses, the thought-producer, he who awakes illusion."

Think about that for a moment, and consider what is being asked. The disciple is not being presented with an option but with a requirement. How many in Blavatsky's day—or even now— would think it possible? How many would even try? How many would attempt it once they understood the enormous difficulties and dangers involved in such an undertaking?

The answers to those questions would consist of three numbers of steadily diminishing proportion. Anyone who has studied the *Voice* has come to that realization already. But HPB believed that there are those who *believe* it can be done, who *are willing* to make the attempt, and who *have the resolve* to face the inevitable trials and difficulties. In short, it is for those brave and stalwart souls— or "the few"—that *The Voice of the Silence* was written.

The Three Fragments

According to H. P. Blavatsky, the three fragments that comprise *The Voice of the Silence* are derived from *The Book of Golden Precepts*, "some of which are pre-Buddhistic while others belong to a later date."[6] In her introduction, she states that the latter work "contains about ninety treatises,"[7] of which she knew thirty-nine from memory. Of those thirty-nine, she chose only three to put before the world in *The Voice of the Silence.*

The title page states that the book is "for the daily use of Lanoos" (*Lanoos* is the Tibetan word for "Disciples"). As such, it uses the familiar metaphor of the path as a way of symbolizing the disciple's progression through a series of stages, described by one commentator as "the first lying beneath one's feet and the last glimmering hardly discernible through the mists of the far distance."[8]

The three fragments are titled "The Voice of the Silence," "The Two Paths," and "The Seven Portals." The first two are preparatory in nature and lead to the third. In his insightful book of essays, *The Creative Silence*, Rohit Mehta suggests that we might better see the continuity of these fragments if we frame them as "The Stage of Preparation," "The Stage of Discovery," and "Treading the Path."[9]

In fragment 1, the disciple is told that before he can hear the One, he must cease "to hear the many." This involves becoming proficient in the practice of Dharana, described by HPB in the glossary as "the intense and perfect concentration of the mind upon some interior object, accompanied by complete abstraction from everything pertaining to the external universe, or the world of the senses." Such a requirement further explains why the *Voice* is for "the few."

In fragment 2, the disciple is urged to examine his motives for embarking upon this journey. He is told about the Open Path versus the Secret Path, the Path of Liberation versus the Path of Woe. He is urged to further sharpen his sense of discernment so that he can distinguish "the real from the false, the ever-fleeting from the everlasting" (vs. 111).

Finally, in fragment 3, the disciple is forewarned of "trials passing speech" (vs. 264), of steep paths that wind uphill, and the need for an "adamantine will"(vs. 201). Although the *Voice* does not gloss over the difficulties, it couples these stern warnings with gentle notes of encouragement such as "hold firm" (vs. 252), "lose not courage" (vs. 272), and "each sincere attempt wins its reward in time" (vs. 274).

HPB: A Perpetual Enigma

The life of H. P. Blavatsky is one shrouded in mystery—mystery at many levels—and one can no more divest her of that element than one could strip innovation from Steve Jobs or distill grandeur and gravitas from the music of Richard Wagner.

In the preface to his book *The Real H. P. Blavatsky,* William Kingsland observes: "The *personality* of H. P. Blavatsky was a very remarkable and complex one. It was in fact a perpetual enigma even to those who knew her most intimately."[10] G. de Purucker echoed this observation in *H. P. Blavatsky, The Mystery:* "[She] was a great psychological mystery to the world of average men. She was a great psychological mystery even to her followers . . . even to those who thought that they knew her best, and who met her daily and worked with her and were taught by her."[11]

Herbert Burrows, a good friend of Blavatsky and eyewitness to the writing of *The Voice of the Silence,* wrote: "Of the real H. P. B. we only caught occasional glimpses. . . . Of her vast and profound knowledge . . . how could one speak?[12] Only its ripples ever reached us, but these would make no ordinary ocean." The penchant of Theosophists to refer to Helena Petrovna Blavatsky simply as HPB is more than a moniker of efficiency whereby one reduces nine syllables and twenty-three letters to a mere three. Even the title page of the original edition of the *Voice* reads "translated and annotated by H.P.B." Why not spell out her entire name as most authors would have done? Another curiosity is the autograph in her personal copy of the *Voice*, which begins, "H.P.B. to H. P. Blavatsky." A first-time reader must surely wonder if these are two separate entities. In an illuminating article published in one of the *American Theosophist* journals, L. Gordon Plummer says, "And here psychology must give way to pneumatology if we are going to understand the difference between H. P. Blavatsky the woman and 'HPB' the teacher."[13] (*Pneumatology* is the study of spiritual beings and phenomena.)

One last question is raised by the second half of the aforementioned autograph, which reads in full: "H.P.B. to H. P. Blavatsky with no kind regards." With no kind regards? How strange is that? Why the apparent show of ingratitude? Fortunately, this is a puzzle that has a plausible answer. In the 1944 edition of the *Voice,* Arya Asanga explains it as "expressing the regret of one who is conscious how the spoken word falls short of the Silent Voice."[14]

A Multifaceted Jewel

Some have compared *The Voice of the Silence* to a precious jewel, and without straining the metaphor we might note that it is a multifaceted one. A skilled lapidary can take a rough stone and transform it into an object of elegance and beauty; the facets of a well-cut gem both capture and disperse the light, creating a visual delight that includes depth and brilliance. The *Voice* is truly a literary gem containing passages of impenetrable depth, as well as of vivid illumination. Like a diamond that has been cut and polished, it is a multifaceted work, which is one of the reasons why it is widely held in such high regard.

Just as a polished gem may be mounted in a ring, pendant, or other suitable setting, the *Voice* is set firmly within the Tibetan Buddhist tradition. This is not to say it is a comprehensive work on Buddhism, but rather that it features elements associated with the Mahayana tradition, e.g., *dharana* (intense concentration), the *paramitas* (supreme virtues), the Doctrine of the Eye versus the Doctrine of the Heart, the Path of Liberation versus the Path of Woe, and others.

In terms of style, one of its notable aspects is the artful employment of poetic imagery. The use of figurative language is not ornamental or contrived but poetry of the highest caliber, being evocative and suggestive, powerful and inspirational.

Another distinct characteristic of this work is its use of paradox. Just as the facets of a well-cut jewel have the ability both to release and to capture the light, the work's poetry serves to illuminate its teachings, at the same time that statements of paradox serve to "hide" the truth within pithy statements that tend to confound the rational mind.

One final aspect deserves mention. Some scholars have observed that the *Voice* is also a book of mysticism. The popular conception of mysticism, however, is often confused and conflated with psychic visions, out-of-body experiences, telepathy, and the like. The validity of the paranormal notwithstanding, true mysticism is a *sui generis*. Its essence is difficult, if not impossible, to convey in words, which probably accounts for the universal tendency of mystics to employ paradox and poetry in their attempts to express the inexpressible.

In summary, *The Voice of the Silence* is a marvelous book of Buddhist teachings enhanced by poetic images, sprinkled with paradoxical aphorisms, and elevated by a sense of genuine mysticism.

The Buddhist Controversy

She was no stranger to controversy: whether it had to do with her psychic phenomena, the letters from Adepts, or her publication of *Isis Unveiled* and *The Secret Doctrine*, controversies dogged Helena Petrovna Blavatsky like paparazzi hound a celebrity. This is not news to those familiar with her life. But what may be unknown is that the 1891 publication of *The Voice of the Silence* also sparked a firestorm, albeit on a smaller scale.

Blavatsky had been accused of being a fraud, of forging letters from the Mahatmas, of fabricating the ideas found in *Isis Unveiled* and *The Secret Doctrine*. The attacks came from many quarters: Christian missionaries, materialistic scientists, status quo apologists—even disgruntled employees at Adyar, the international center of the Theosophical Society. But the animus aimed at the *Voice* came from a rather select and erudite group: Western Buddhist scholars who stated smugly and confidently that it absolutely did not contain any real Buddhist teachings.

Today—more than 120 years later—nobody questions that the *Voice* contains sublime expressions of Tibetan Buddhist teachings. Within this limited space, two examples as to why this is so may be given: In 1928, William Kingsland published *The Real H. P. Blavatsky*; it contained a footnote explaining that a recent Chinese edition of the *Voice* had been endorsed by the Tashi Lama as being "the only true exposition in English of the Heart Doctrine of *Mahayana* Buddhism, and its noble idea of self-sacrifice for humanity."[15] Forty-five years later, Joy Mills and Helen Zahara, while attending the 97th International Theosophical Convention in Adyar, made a side trip to visit the Dalai Lama in Dharamsala. After discussing *The Voice of the Silence*, His Holiness commented that its contents were quite "authentic."

So, what provoked the dispute among Buddhist scholars? The answer, I think, is fairly easy to explain. At the close of the nineteenth century, most Westerners viewed Tibet as a remote and backward country; few had been there, and information about its people and its culture was scant. Western scholars were familiar with Theravada Buddhism, which was found in southern Asia, an area that was much more accessible. In truth, one can hardly blame them for their ignorance as to the lamaistic teachings from the north. It was not until much later, when Westerners freely traveled to Nepal and Tibet and after the Chinese Communist invasion of Tibet in the 1950s, that knowledge of Tibetan Buddhism became widespread. Although some of the controversies surrounding HPB are still parroted by lazy authors, the original debate over the *Voice* has long since faded into the Hall of Silence, a place history reserves for the misinformed opinions and widely discredited judgments of so-called experts.

Paprika, Oregano, and Literary Condiments

Spiritual books from the East often employ a literary device in which the teachings are put forth ostensibly as a dialogue between a wise guru and an aspiring devotee. We find this to some extent in *The Crest Jewel of Wisdom* but much more so in the Bhagavad Gita, where Arjuna and Krishna engage in an ongoing conversation. Not unexpectedly, *The Voice of the Silence* also makes limited use of this convention by framing its teachings as a discussion between a humble but worthy disciple (*lanoo*) and an enlightened preceptor. An intriguing aspect of this stylistic practice is the use of monikers (or nicknames) to designate the pupil. Arjuna, for example, is referred to as Pāndava, Bhārata, son of Kuntī, slayer of demons, conqueror of sleep, and many other appellations. Although the use of sobriquets may at first create confusion in the mind of the reader, their real purpose is to add clarity and depth by revealing something significant about the disciple or the transformative process.

The first fragment of the *Voice* is essentially a monologue in which the guru is speaking to the lanoo, whose presence is implied, not stated. I found this to be an interesting parallel to the practice of the ancient Pythagorean School in which the student was required to listen in silence during the probationary period of training. But the tacit presence of the pupil does not prevent his guru from addressing him by various monikers, some of which are quite colorful, a habit that he continues throughout the second and third fragments.

All told, my audit of the *Voice* identified at least three dozen such monikers. Some paint him as a rank novice (*beginner, ignorant disciple*), while those used in the third fragment foretell higher levels of spiritual attainment (*Arhan, Bodhisattva, Master of Samadhi*). Some point to requisite qualities that the disciple must develop (*fearless warrior, thou of patient heart*), while others intimate the nature of trials that lie ahead (*pursuer of truth, slayer of thy thoughts, perceiver of external shadows*). The first-time reader may glide over these subtleties without notice, but they are there, all the same. Some may be tempted to dismiss them as nothing more than ornamentation, as in the use of melodic trills in Baroque music. But I would prefer a different metaphor, likening them to the paprika on a macaroni and cheese casserole, the bay leaves in soup, or the oregano in spaghetti sauce—all of which augment the main course by adding subtle but deeply satisfying flavors. As ideas are said to be food for the mind, the analogy is hopefully not too far-fetched.

The Poignant Poetry of H. P. Blavatsky

It has been said that the poetry in *The Voice of the Silence* is as exquisite as its paradoxes are startling. By *poetry* is meant the artful use of language to create poetic imagery. Such images are formed when two unlike objects sharing like attributes are compared, as in the case of a person who is said to be in the twilight of his career. What connects twilight and career are endings; twilight comes at the end of the day, and all careers inevitably come to an end. One example of poetic imagery found in the *Voice*, "thy dark garments of illusion" (vs. 33), compares ignorance to a piece of dark (and possibly heavy) clothing; one serves to cover the body, the other to veil the mind.

In the preface, Mme. Blavatsky says: "I have done my best to preserve the poetical beauty of language and imagery which characterize the original." We should not overlook or discount the power of poetry in this work. To underscore this point, let us state a simple fact: *The mind is subject to illusion*—a statement that is as unremarkable and forgettable as it is undeniably true. But under HPB's skillful pen, this trite maxim becomes something else:

> For the mind is like a mirror; it gathers dust while it reflects. It needs the gentle breezes of Soul-Wisdom to brush away the dust of our illusions (vs. 115).

Here the prejudices and biases of the human mind are compared to dust settling on a mirror, one that becomes less and less able to reflect the light, just as a conditioned mind is less able to perceive and express the truth without bias and distortion. The simple beauty of the language serves to elevate a pedestrian truth to a memorable statement of enduring inspiration. However, HPB takes the same truth—*the mind is subject to illusion*—and articulates it very differently in the following passage:

> The moth attracted to the dazzling flame of thy night-lamp is doomed to perish in the viscid oil. The unwary soul that fails to grapple with the mocking demon of illusion, will return to earth the slave of Mara (vs. 35).

The change of tone is as unmistakable as a melody that is played first in a major, and then in a minor, key. The mood shifts from one of quiet reflection to one of stern admonishment; and HPB does this solely through her choice of imagery. From the contemplation of dust gathering quietly on a mirror, we now envision the stark image of dying moths entrapped in hot, viscid oil. The underlying truth is the same in both verses, but the dramatic effect created by poetic imagery could not be more dissimilar. Careful readers will take time to savor the powerful wordplay found in the *Voice*, thus enhancing their delight and enjoyment of this little masterpiece.

Defining *Paradox*

The Voice of the Silence has one thing in common with some of the world's scriptures, which is the presence of paradoxical statements. Although the word *paradox* has more than one meaning, it generally includes two elements: a contradiction and an element of truth. Someone with a delightful sense of humor once said that a paradox is a truth standing on its head in order to grab our attention. The contradiction is what attracts our attention; the hidden kernel of truth is what holds it.

Without attempting a comprehensive treatise on the nature of paradox, we might consider a few of its common usages. One instance would be when the term is used to describe a person possessing seemingly contradictory qualities. For example, Robert DeNiro is a consummate actor who has appeared in many films but also has a reputation for being very shy when not in front of a camera. Another example would be a statement that is contrary to received opinion, as in Isaiah 45:7: "I form light and create darkness, I make peace and create evil; I the Lord do all these things." Most Christians conveniently overlook this biblical passage, since Christian orthodoxy attributes evil to Satan, not God. A third type of paradox would be a statement that seems opposed to reason and common sense but yet might be true. For instance, in the Bhagavad Gita Krishna tells Arjuna, "He who perceives inaction in action, and action in inaction, is wise among men."[16] On the surface this statement seems nonsensical, but when one understands that action includes movements of the mind, Krishna's words have profound meaning. The *Tao Te Ching* has this enigmatic statement:

"The farther one goes, the less one knows."[17] This is paradoxical because conventional wisdom equates experience ("the farther one goes") with an increase in knowledge. One is reminded of Seneca's epigram: "To be everywhere is to be nowhere."[18]

So as not to deprive the reader the joy of discovering the marvelous paradoxes in *The Voice of the Silence*, I will mention just one: "Thou canst not travel on the Path until thou hast become that Path itself" (vs. 58). On one level, this statement seems illogical. The conflict is resolved, however, when we realize that a psychological point is being made. The neophyte cannot "travel on the Path" as though taking a walk in the park, or a stroll along the beach, and then return home unchanged. There has to be a total commitment, a transformation of one's inner nature, and *then* one gradually becomes a living embodiment of that path.

The Limited Utility of Language

In her preface, Blavatsky states that *The Voice of the Silence* is dedicated to "the few real mystics in the Theosophical Society." For a book bearing that title, it should come as no surprise that within its pages are to be found elements of mysticism. But before going further, perhaps we should discuss what is meant by that term.

In an article by Beatrice Bruteau entitled "The Validity of Mysticism," the author begins with this cautionary note: "The word *mysticism* has been so misused that it is best to clear first what it does not mean."[19] She then provides a long list of items that mysticism is *not*, including telepathy, out-of-body experiences, miracles, and revelations from saints, angels, or discarnate entities. Evelyn Underhill, in her book *Mystics of the Church*, notes that the terms *mystic* and *mysticism* "are generally so vaguely and loosely used that they convey no precise meaning to our minds, and have now come to be perhaps the most ambiguous terms in the whole vocabulary of religion."[20] Even today, the terms *mysticism* and *mystic* are still tossed about in the media by pundits and commentators who have absolutely no idea of what those words mean.

In her book *Practical Mysticism,* Underhill gives as good a definition as any as to what these terms mean: "Mysticism is the art of union with Reality. The mystic is a person who has attained that union in greater or less degree; or who aims at and believes in such attainment."[21] Bruteau, in the article cited above, offers a more compact definition: "To realize oneself as 'one with the One' is mysticism." Two passages from the *Voice* carrying mystical overtones come to mind: "Seek in the impersonal for the Eternal Man" (vs. 116) and "That which is uncreate abides in thee, disciple" (vs. 33).

The mystical elements found in *The Voice* are often seen at first glance as being paradoxical, two examples being "the soundless sound" (vs. 2) or "now thy self is lost in Self" (vs. 90). But how long can one pontificate about "the soundless sound" before sounding vacuous and pretentious? As Bruteau rightly points out: "We are pretending to talk about something that is by definition incommunicable. . . . We are in the realm of the paradoxical for our language and logic."[22]

When dealing with mysticism, therefore, words are of limited utility. To understand mysticism truly is not a matter of words but of *experience*, for it deals with aspects of consciousness that are transcendent, indescribable, and incommunicable. The language of empiricism is ill suited for expressing the subtle, inexpressible realities of mystical consciousness. This is why it has been said that the language of mysticism consists of poetry and paradox, two modes often used to express the inexpressible; and, as we have learned, these two elements are to be found in abundance throughout *The Voice of the Silence.*

Chapter 11

REFLECTIONS ON *THE VOICE OF THE SILENCE*

Becoming the Path

Thou canst not travel on the Path before thou hast become that Path itself (vs. 58).

What is the meaning of the above puzzling statement? What does it mean to *become* the path? Why is this effort required before setting one's foot upon it?

As a metaphor, the image of a path is used in widely different contexts: a university student nearing graduation envisions her career path; a business owner conceives a pathway for expanding his company; a nutritionist devises a pathway to health for a client; a Hollywood agent calculates a pathway to success for a young, aspiring actress. In each example there is a series of steps leading to a desired end.

The difference is that the path spoken of in Theosophical literature such as *The Voice of the Silence* is not a means to an end—it is a way of life. It is based not on self-interest but on altruism. It is based not on self-gain but on service to others. The aspirant who has entered this path of service has made a solemn decision, one that will result in profound changes, both internal and external. Mme. Blavatsky described it thus: "There is a road, steep and thorny, beset with perils of every kind, but yet a road, and it leads to the very heart of the universe."[1] She then speaks of a secret gateway that "opens inward only, and closes fast behind the neophyte for evermore."[2] Everything she says indicates that the decision to travel this road is not one to be taken lightly.

A college graduate may pursue a career in her chosen field, but doing so does not require a fundamental change in personality. By contrast, the neophyte entering the path is told to "cleanse thy mind-body and make clean thy heart." No easy task. The owner of a small business may walk away from his failing enterprise and start another. The pilgrims traveling the path do not have that option. Though they may stumble and lose their way, they are told to "fight on and to the charge return again, and yet again" (vs. 272). A skillful actress can play a multitude of parts and yet be somebody entirely different in her private life. Unlike the actress or actor, the disciple must forgo artifice and facades and is instructed to "divest thyself of thy dark garments of illusion" (vs. 18).

So, to return to my original questions, what is the meaning of the enigmatic citation quoted above? Why can we not travel that path before we have become that path? A brief clue is provided by Joy Mills in her book of commentary, *From Inner to Outer Transformation:* "We are not separate from the path, from the process."[3] I think what Joy is saying is that the process of self-transformation requires a total commitment on the part of the aspirant. The struggle is between the higher Self and the lower self, and a half-hearted effort will not be enough to succeed. There must be a willingness and a conscious determination to shine the light of the Spirit on every aspect of our personality. We cannot stand to the side as a neutral observer, without fully investing ourselves in the process. In a very real sense, we have to *become* the path, for it is a process that takes place within ourselves.

The Limitations of the Mind

The mind is the great slayer of the Real (vs. 4).

Perhaps no other verse from *The Voice of the Silence* has been so often quoted yet so little understood as the one above. Some have assumed it to be a denigration of the mind; others, that the training and development of mental faculties are unimportant. That is a misreading of the text. The mind is a marvelous instrument, and it is what distinguishes human beings from animals.

There are times, however, when the mind works against us. Many years ago, I was studying music at the University of Wisconsin. I loved classical music and had purchased season tickets for the Milwaukee Symphony. To my dismay, I didn't enjoy any of the concerts. Why? I had assumed that learning about harmony, counterpoint, and orchestration would enhance my listening experience, but, instead of enhancing my enjoyment of the music, my newly acquired knowledge got in the way. I tried to analyze everything and enjoyed nothing.

Again, the mind is a marvelous instrument for dealing with the realities of this world, but there are limits to what it can do. Mystics speak of another reality, one that is beyond this world of appearances, one that eludes the senses. In the Mundaka Upanishad, we read, "The eye cannot see it; the mind cannot grasp it."[4] And in *The Secret Doctrine*, Blavatsky says, "It transcends the power of human conception and could only be dwarfed by any human expression or similitude" (1: 14).

One of the things that the mind does exceedingly well is to classify and categorize. That is obviously a very useful function: who would want to do business with a pharmacist who is ambivalent about labels? On the other hand, Krishnamurti once noted that "naming is a very convenient way of disposing of things and of people."[5] To assume that we understand something *merely* by assigning it a label or a category is therefore to engage in self-delusion:

> The Tao that can be told is not the eternal Tao.
> The name that can be named is not the eternal name.[6]

Yogis and sages train themselves to withdraw their consciousness from this sensory world and enter another one, a world that is more real, they say, than this one. They speak of becoming one with God, Brahman, or the Ground of all Being. Such experiences are all but indescribable. In speaking about the unfathomable peace therein, Thomas Merton says, "As soon as you attempt to make words or thoughts about it, you are excluded."[7] And it is in this way, I believe, that the mind becomes the slayer of the Real.

The Power of Discernment

*Before thou takest thy first step, learn to discern the real
from the false, the ever-fleeting from the everlasting* (vs. 111).

Before the neophyte takes the first step on the path, he is advised by an experienced teacher to develop the power of discrimination, the basic function of which is to draw distinctions or perceive differences. The Sanskrit word for this is *viveka*, broadly defined as the ability to distinguish between the real and the unreal. The word *discernment* has also been used, as has the word *insight*. In any case, this advice is a veritable sine qua non for those seriously considering the path of discipleship, and it has been so since time immemorial.

To better understand the function of the discriminative faculty in the spiritual life, it may be helpful to cite a few examples from ordinary life. A world-class chef, for instance, has developed the ability to distinguish between subtle flavors and knows when an entrée has too much basil and not enough oregano. A skillful painter knows the exact shade of color and degree of brightness needed in order to convey a certain mood or impression from the canvas. The conductor of a symphony orchestra has an acute sense of when the tempo is too fast or too slow, whether the crescendo of the brass section is overpowering or understated. We admire such artists for their well-developed esthetic sensibilities and their percipient sensitivity to subtle nuances.

The power of discernment plays a key role in the spiritual life as well. It enables the aspirant to discern the true from the false, the important from the unimportant, the eternal from the ephemeral, and other such dualities. Its application to the inner life depends not on sensory organs—a discerning eye, ear, or palate—but on right perception, which is to say, one's understanding of the world. We are told that the objective world is not what it appears to be, a point on which scientists and sages agree. So important is this recognition that, in Buddhism, the very first step of the Noble Eightfold Path is listed as Right View. If the disciple does not view the world rightly, he will trip and stumble on the path or lose his way in an endless series of byways and cul-de-sacs. While "the path" may be a familiar metaphor that rolls easily off the tongue, the pitfalls and dangers associated with this process are most real, and sometimes unexpected. And so, in *The Voice of the Silence,* the seeker is forewarned: "This earth, disciple, is the Hall of Sorrow, wherein are set along the path of dire probations, traps to ensnare thy Ego" (vs. 17).

I May Be Ignorant, but I'm Not Stupid

Shun ignorance (vs. 116).

If my neighbor refers to me as being ignorant, it is safe to assume that he is not paying me a compliment and that he believes me to be a rather obtuse and dull-witted fellow. While that may be true prior to my having had my morning cup of coffee, any thesaurus will tell you that ignorance is not necessarily a synonym for stupidity; it may also refer to a lack of knowledge or being uninformed about something. In that sense, I willingly and unabashedly confess my total ignorance of calculus, nuclear physics, the techniques of international bond trading, the fifty words that the Inuit have for snow, or one hundred other areas of knowledge that have little or no relevance to my life. But, if my neighbor uses that epithet *after* I've had my cup of coffee . . .

The dialogue that takes place throughout the *Voice* is between an enlightened guru and an inquiring lanoo. In addressing the lanoo, the guru uses a variety of epithets, including beginner, neophyte, and *ignorant disciple*. Hopefully, the lanoo has not yet had his morning cup of coffee and therefore takes no offense.

In the first two fragments of the *Voice*, the disciple is told that he must avoid ignorance, a point that is made repeatedly and is therefore of some importance. Today's aspirant may ask, "What *kind* of ignorance am I to avoid?" A search on Google reveals various categories of ignorance, the number of which depends on your point of view: Catholic theology lists three; the Kabbalah lists four; Sri Aurobindo, in his book *The Life Divine*, lists seven. Since *The Voice of the Silence* is a book of inspiration and not a treatise, it does not provide us with a neat and orderly system of classification, but it does contain a number of memorable passages encouraging the use of discernment when it comes to understanding the nature of the material world, what it means to be human, and the nature of the Self.

So the word *ignorance* as used in *The Voice of the Silence* is not a pejorative moniker but refers simply to the state of being unaware or of lacking a certain type of knowledge. As for my neighbor, the next time he refers to me as ignorant, I may have to loan him my thesaurus.

The Captivating Spell of Illusion

Shun ignorance, and likewise shun illusion (vs. 116).

The frequent number of references to illusion found in *The Voice of the Silence* indicates that disciples who ignore it do so at their peril. For example, we are told to be wary of the "sweet-tongued voices of illusion" (vs. 31), which have the power to cast a spell over the mind and lead one astray. Everybody has experienced illusion in some form or another, but few care to admit how susceptible they may be to its power. The comforting notion that, somehow, I am immune and that it is the other guy who lives inside a "castle of illusion" (vs. 14) is, in itself, a type of illusion.

The Secret Doctrine states: "Māyā or illusion is an element which enters into all finite things" (1:39). A few examples may demonstrate the veracity of that statement. Imagine a busy salesman who's been calling on customers all day; now he's relaxing at home, exhausted, sitting quietly in his favorite easy chair. Has he stopped moving? No, he's moving through space at 67,000 miles per hour—and so is everything else on the planet as it orbits the sun. The power of illusion is sometimes used to create a deliberate effect, such as a short man wearing a suit with vertical pin stripes so as to appear taller, or a tall thin man wearing a sweater with horizontal stripes so as to give the appearance of heft.

Some people may think of illusions as merely phantasies or fancies, whereas they are often orderly phenomena following the laws of nature. The sudden drop in pitch of a siren on a passing ambulance is an example of the Doppler Effect. Snell's Law explains the familiar optical illusion created by beams of light as they pass through water or glass.

In Buddhist literature, it has long been a commonplace that the material world is not the solid, permanent reality that it appears to be. The Diamond Sutra states, "All that has form is an illusory existence."[8] The Dhammapada advises, "Look on the world as a bubble, look on it as a mirage."[9] Discoveries in modern physics support these ancient views, as science has proven that the physical atom consists of far more empty space than actual substance. And so *The Voice of the Silence* advises the spiritual aspirant to meditate on the impermanence of all physical forms until they appear as unreal as those forms and images appearing in dreams.

The Illusion of Death

Before the soul can see, the harmony within must be attained, and fleshly eyes be rendered blind to all illusion (vs. 9).

One of the most persistently powerful illusions to which human beings remain susceptible is the notion that death is something to be feared. The reality of death—in all its forms—is evident enough, but most people prefer not to think about it. Whether their outlook on life is religious or secular, spiritualistic or materialistic, everybody knows that death is inevitable, yet we seldom talk about it. Avoiding conversations about death is not going to make it any less certain. To understand the process of death, we need to ask *what* it is that actually dies. What is it that comes to an end? *The Voice of the Silence* refers to the self of matter and the Self of Spirit, a juxtaposition that points to a profound paradox of human existence—mortal frames of flesh infused with the vibrant life of immortal Spirit: one is temporal, the other timeless; one is finite, the other infinite; one is subject to a multitude of limitations, the other is a storehouse of unlimited potential. Whichever of these two realities we identify with will strongly influence our attitude toward death.

As individuals, it is normal to view life from a limited perspective; we become immersed in the flow of our life, along with its particular set of circumstances, its unique challenges, its golden opportunities. To see with the eyes of the Spirit, however, is to view life through a much broader lens, one that reveals our deep inner connection to our neighbors, our community, and, indeed, all of humanity. But how often does that happen? In the same way that the smudged lens of a telescope obscures our vision, the existence of inner conflict and personal bias prevents us from perceiving the world as it really is. To see things as they truly are requires a transcendence of the personal self. If we are in a state of psychological turmoil, we tend to see the whole world as being in conflict. If we are selfish and egotistical, we tend to see those qualities mirrored in the behavior of others.

The *Voice of the Silence* encourages us to identify with the self of Spirit, for that is our true identity. The personal self, we are told, has no more real substance than does a shadow. When we identify with the Self of Spirit—that immortal spark within each and every one of us—we no longer dread the prospect of dying. Death then is seen as the end of a chapter, not the end of the book. "Thy shadows live and vanish: that which in thee shall live forever . . . is not of fleeting life" (vs. 138).

Illusion and Delusion

When to himself his form appears unreal . . . (vs. 6)

John Ruskin, the Victorian art critic and a contemporary of H. P. Blavatsky, said, "To see clearly is poetry, prophecy, and religion all in one."[10] It seems to me that Ruskin's observation can be related to spirituality. A truly spiritual life—and not one that is merely pious or perfunctory—contains not only great depth and intense devotion but acute clarity of vision. By clarity of vision, I'm not suggesting the seeing of angels and auras and halos, but rather the ability to distinguish between the peripheral and the essential, the personal and the impersonal, the passing and the timeless. In the old Sanskrit writings, the sages describe this ability with the term *viveka*, for which the English translation is "discriminative wisdom." For the person living a sanctified life, seeing clearly must surely reveal the beauty of life, the oneness of life, and the arc of evolutionary unfoldment.

In HPB's wonderful spiritual guidebook, *The Voice of the Silence*, the ability to see clearly is one of the preliminary requirements put forth. Again and again, the aspirant is warned of two dangers, *illusion* and *delusion*, both of which involve a distortion in the perception of reality, thus masking the truth of what is. While illusions involve distortions deriving from outer conditions (i.e., the appearance of a nonexistent oasis in the distant desert sands), delusions involve those arising from the mind itself (the notion, say, that I am the reincarnation of Napoleon, Caesar, or John the Baptist, depending on what day of the week it happens to be). Both are potential pitfalls that must be recognized and overcome.

According to the *Voice,* if the disciple identifies with his or her physical body (referred to as the *form*); if he thinks himself to be this temporary personality (referred to as a passing *shadow*); if she shrinks from pain and sighs for pleasure (revealing a lack of inner equilibrium); if he sees himself as the center of the universe (whether unconsciously or not); then the disciple truly "is caught in the webs of delusion" and must struggle to be free of these "dark garments" before proceeding on the path. When this has been accomplished and clarity of vision established, "then to the inner ear will speak THE VOICE OF THE SILENCE" (vs. 13).

The "Great Heresy"

This earth, disciple, is the Hall of Sorrow, wherein are set along
the path of dire probations, traps to ensnare thy Ego
by the delusion called Great Heresy (vs.17).

The word *heresy* carries the negative connotations of intolerance, zealotry, and persecution; its appearance in a book on compassion such as *The Voice of the Silence* is therefore somewhat startling and unexpected. Before we examine the above passage, let us consider some examples of how the term is used. In politics, an elected official who dares to voice an opinion contrary to party doctrine risks being branded as heretical. A scientist who takes a position contrary to the one embraced by the scientific establishment may find that his funding and promotional opportunities disappear. Public speakers have been known to facetiously preface an unconventional opinion with, "I hope you don't accuse me of heresy, but. . . ."

It is no laughing matter, however, to be accused of religious heresy when the consequences may be—and often have been—not only condemnation and ostracism, but imprisonment, torture, and death. Victims of the Christian Inquisition included Galileo, Joan of Arc, and Giordano Bruno. Today, the mullahs in Iran view the Baha'i faith as heretical. Most Orthodox Jews consider Reform Judaism to be heretical. Many more examples could be cited, but the point is that charges of heresy are not the exclusive province of any one religion.

In what sense, then, is the word *heresy* used in the above citation from the *Voice?* Is it used to describe a dissent from a dominant theory or doctrine? Is it used to describe a disagreement with the status quo? Is it used to describe a deviation from religious opinion or church dogma? No, it is used in none of those ways. In a gloss to the above verse, Mme. Blavatsky explains that "Great Heresy" refers to the belief that the self, or soul, exists separately from the one universal Self. On the path of compassion, it is a fundamental requirement to see that our life is interconnected with all other lives, that we do not live in a vacuum, that our thoughts and actions have consequences in the lives of others. The *Voice* prods the reader with poignant passages, such as, "Hast thou attuned thy heart and mind to the great heart mind and heart of all mankind?" (vs. 225). Or this call to action: "Let not the fierce sun dry one tear of pain before thyself hast wiped it from the sufferer's eye" (vs. 60). Or this short but powerful maxim: "Compassion is no attribute. It is the Law of laws" (vs. 300). To be deluded by selfishness, greed, and narcissism is to violate the universal law of compassion.

A Prison of Our Own Making

If thy soul smiles while bathing in the sunlight of thy life;
if thy soul sings within her chrysalis of flesh and matter;
if thy soul weeps inside her castle of illusion;
if thy soul struggles to break the silver thread that binds her
to the Master, know, O disciple, thy soul is of the earth (vs. 14).

In the above passage, the disciple is presented with a set of four conditions and is asked to consider whether any of them apply. If the fledgling disciple is honest, he will most likely identify with one or more of them, taking that recognition as an indication of more work to be done in terms of self-transformation. One cannot become a "Walker of the Sky" (vs. 40) or ride the great "Bird of Life" (vs. 20) if one's soul is bound by earthly interests. Let us now consider the four scenarios given and how they may be interpreted.

The first two phrases from the above citation represent pleasure (smiling and singing), while the latter two represent pain (weeping and struggling). Pleasure and pain are often referred to in Eastern philosophy as one example in the pairs of opposites. These are polarities that all human beings experience, often alternating between them like the pendulum of a clock. Unfortunately, if our personal happiness depends on outer circumstances, i.e., those times when everything seems to be going in our favor, then it rests upon shaky ground. Moreover, when we allow ourselves to become self-absorbed in our cocoon of self-interest, oblivious to the world and the concerns of others, then our so-called happiness is indeed fragile and tenuous. In terms of pain, we often experience acute suffering when reality intrudes upon the illusions we have eagerly embraced and nurtured over time. To live in a "castle of illusion" is to live in a veritable prison of our own making.

Lastly, the reference to breaking the "silver thread" refers to the epic struggle between the personal and higher Self, a formidable battle that every disciple without exception must face.

To be earthbound is to be vulnerable to the push and pull of pleasure and pain, forever tossed to and fro by these agents of desire, unable to rise above one's personal nature and enter the hall of wisdom "wherein all shadows are unknown, and where the light of truth shines with unfading glory" (vs. 32). This is the reason why many spiritual guidebooks emphasize the necessity of developing nonattachment, discernment, and self-control.

Affirming Our Own Humanity

Let not the fierce sun dry one tear of pain
before thyself hast wiped it from the sufferer's eye (vs. 60).

The above passage has to be one of the more poignant (and challenging) from the *Voice,* an irresistible call to compassionate action that speaks directly to the heart. Whether one is a Buddhist or a Christian, a Muslim or a Jew, an atheist or an agnostic, the emotional appeal of this passage is undeniable. Any sensitive person will find their heart stirred, not only by an exquisitely fashioned line of poetry *about* human suffering, but by *its actual presence.* But instead of being aware of those tears, we submerge ourselves in the predictable routine of going to work, chauffeuring the kids to soccer, preparing that client presentation, scheduling our doctor appointments, and so on. We become overwhelmed by all these demands and obligations, some of which we create ourselves, others of which are put upon us by family, friends, our boss, or society in general. The distinct danger is that we end up wrapping ourselves in a cocoon of self-interest and self-involvement, thereby growing oblivious to the pain of those around us, especially those who are

not a part of our immediate circle. This is one reason why the call
to compassion is so challenging. Swept away as we often are by the
centripetal movement of our busy lives, we fail to see the ubiquitous tears of suffering, allowing them to dry—neglected, ignored,
and exposed—in the fierce light of day.

Sometimes we tend to overthink things that in reality are really
quite simple. Being compassionate, for example, does not require
you to solve all of the world's problems; no one has the time, energy, or resources to do that. But you can respond on a case-by-case
basis to situations as they arise throughout your day, often requir-
ing no more than a kind word, a sympathetic ear, or a loving smile.
The person who suffers usually does not ask you to solve his or her
problems, but rather to listen and sympathize. You and I can do
that, provided we remain alert and observant. As we proceed with
our busy lives, let us remember that wiping away the tears of another is not an inconvenience or distraction—it is an affirmation
of our common bond of humanity. When we recognize that salient
fact of nature, we also affirm our own humanity.

A Sobering Thought

*The selfish devotee lives to no purpose. The man who does not go
through his appointed work in life—has lived in vain* (vs. 153).

Although these two sentences are aimed at disciples, it may be
profitable to consider the second in a more general context, asking
ourselves what lessons it may hold for us—not as devotees of a particular path or school of thought, but in the broader sense of simply being receptive to wisdom, regardless of where it may be found.

Taking it at face value, the second sentence tells us three things:
(1) we have a purpose for being here; (2) once we acknowledge that
purpose, we need to act upon it; (3) if we fail to act accordingly, we

will have squandered the opportunities of this incarnation.

Who can say what purpose this particular incarnation holds for you? Unfortunately, no one can provide you with that information. The truth is that you have to discover it for yourself. While it is a fact that some individuals find their purpose early in life, others struggle for years before getting a sense of what theirs might be. Sadly, there are those who never seem to find it, perhaps being ignorant of the fact that their life *does* have a purpose beyond just making a living and getting by. One can surmise from watching and observing that the vast majority of people fall within this category. It is unfortunate, because without this knowledge we are simply drifting along the currents of life—getting out of bed in the morning, going through the motions, carrying out the daily routines—but with no real understanding of where we are going, other than chasing some illusive and ephemeral measure of happiness.

The above citation suggests that if we avoid our life's designated work, we will have lived in vain. That is a very sobering thought and one that should give us pause. Yet we may wonder if this passage should be taken literally. If we don't find our life's purpose, will we *really* have lived in vain? Perhaps this warning is meant for those who *know* their purpose but *fail* to pursue it. Another possibility is that the author of the *Voice* is simply using hyperbole for effect. It's difficult to imagine a life from which nothing useful could be salvaged. In any event, the reality is that each incarnation involves a finite amount of time. What we do with that limited amount of time is something for which Karma will hold us accountable.

Stay the Course

Have perseverance as one who doth for evermore endure (vs. 138).

The Voice of the Silence makes no attempt to minimize the challenges associated with treading the path. Its vivid descriptions of the potential pitfalls faced by the aspirant may seem exaggerated to some, especially if they have had no experience with that way of life. Still others may feel discouraged, or even intimidated, by stark admonitions such as "long and weary is the way before thee" (vs. 74), or "the more thou dost advance, the more thy feet pitfalls will meet" (vs. 239). However, the text also contains passages marked by buoyant enthusiasm, such as "the more one dares, the more he shall obtain" (ibid.), or "each sincere attempt wins its reward in time" (vs. 274). Throughout the book, a judicious balance is struck between sober words of caution and those conveying cheerful optimism.

Perseverance is universally considered to be an admirable quality and for good reason. Without it, we are likely to fall short of attaining our goals or realizing our most cherished dreams. Lacking perseverance, a budding author fails to find a publisher for her first book and forgoes a promising career; a talented young actor becomes discouraged after a few failed auditions and settles for a boring day job; an overconfident and unprepared high-school senior scores poorly on the college SAT test, thus limiting her options for college. By any measure of worldly success, perseverance is without a doubt an essential character trait, but its usefulness in the life of the spiritual aspirant is also not to be overlooked or diminished.

Drawing on the Mahayana Buddhist tradition, the *Voice* instructs the disciple to master the *paramitas*, or supreme virtues. If my mind is accustomed to drifting from one thought to another, it is a safe bet that I will have difficulty with *dharana* (intense concentration). If the love of instant gratification and desire for quick results describes my personality, it should be no surprise that I will have difficulty mastering *kshanti* (unruffled patience). If I am overly sensitive and bristle at the least critical remark, then I will struggle learning *vairāgya* (indifference to pleasure and pain). The force of habit is strong, and I may grow weary in my efforts.

Originally, I may have been motivated by high spiritual ideals, but the magnitude of the task raises doubts, and, like the poet John Keats, I may sigh with resignation:

> Bright star, would I were steadfast as thou art.

In moments like this, it would be well to recall these encouraging words from the *Voice*:

> That which in thee shall live ever . . . is not of fleeting life: it is the man that was, that is, and will be, and for whom the hour shall never strike (vs. 138).

Nature, Part 1

Become as one with Nature's Soul-Thought (vs. 249).

The word *nature* appears thirteen times in *The Voice of the Silence*—the preface and glossary not included—and the shades and nuances of meaning it carries vary with the context. Considering the importance that the concept of nature plays in Theosophical literature (the index of *The Secret Doctrine* contains over ninety references to nature, while that of *The Key to Theosophy* contains twenty-three), an examination of how it is used in the *Voice* is not just an academic exercise but a useful step toward gaining greater appreciation and understanding.

As a frame of reference, we may first consider what philosophers throughout history have said about nature. Although a variety of meanings have been attributed to it, *The Oxford Companion to Philosophy* lists three as particularly noteworthy. Nature is considered:

1. Everything that there is in the physical world of experience . . . the universe and its contents, in short.
2. The living world (past and present) as opposed to the non-living.

3. That [view] which sees everything, especially the organic world, set off against humans and the consequences of their labors.

For another perspective, we might refer to *Merriam-Webster's Collegiate Dictionary*, which defines nature as "the inherent character or constitution of a person or thing; disposition, temperament; a creative and controlling force in the universe; natural scenery." And for still another view, we may consider three statements by Blavatsky:

1. Everything in the universe, throughout all its kingdoms, is conscious (1:274).
2. When we speak of the Deity and make it identical, hence coeval, with nature, the eternal and uncreate nature is meant, and not your aggregate of flitting shadows and finite unrealities.[11]
3. Nature may err, and often does.[12]

Which of these definitions or meanings of nature are applicable to *The Voice of the Silence?* We will continue this discussion in the next essay.

Nature, Part 2

Chafe not at Karma nor at Nature's changeless laws (vs. 65).

What are commonly referred to as "the laws of the land," though necessary for the smooth functioning of a civil society, are in fact mutable, sometimes arbitrary, and often circumscribed, which is to say, limited in jurisdiction to the city, state, or nation that has adopted them. Nature's laws bear none of those characteristics, being neither transitory, nor whimsical, nor parochial. The law of gravity works no differently in Barcelona than in Salt Lake City, nor can its force be repealed by a tyrant or amended by any legislative body or head of state. If you jump off the Golden Gate Bridge, gravity does its work and does not discriminate on the basis of your age, gender, or social standing.

John Stuart Mill, in his essay "On Nature," offers some insights that are apropos:

> No word is more commonly associated with the word "nature" than "law"; and this last word has distinctly two meanings, in one of which it denotes some definite portion of what is, in the other of what ought to be. We speak of the law of gravitation, the three laws of motion, the law of definite proportions in chemical combination, the vital laws of organized beings. All these are portions of what is. We also speak of criminal law, the civil law, the law of honor, the law of veracity, the law of justice; all of which are portions of what ought to be, or of somebody's suppositions, feelings, or commands respecting what ought to be.[13]

We may complain about man-made laws that we dislike or that seem unjust, but these laws can be changed, improved, or even done away with. By contrast, the laws of nature are eternal, immutable, and impartial. Through centuries of careful observation and testing, scientists have discovered and given names to a great many of them. Mill describes these laws as "neither more nor less than the observed uniformities in the occurrence of phenomena; partly uniformities of antecedence and sequence, partly of concomitance."[14]

Theosophy informs us that there are subtle realms of nature, undetectable even by the amazing instruments of modern science. These unseen worlds are also governed by laws, often described in our literature as occult, or hidden. Their existence has been perceived by the ancient Rishis and Yogis, who, through intense training in yogic disciplines, utilized the highest faculties of human consciousness to probe this unseen dimension of nature. And one of the foundational laws that they discovered is called Karma.

In a grand and sweeping statement, Blavatsky described Karma as "the Ultimate Law of the Universe, the source, the origin and the fount of all other laws which exist throughout Nature."[15] If such a statement moves us to deep reflection, perhaps the most appropriate response would be one of awe, wonder, and humility.

Nature, Part 3

Nature's strongest mights possess
no power to stay thy course (vs. 264).

If the laws of nature are immutable and their operation universal and impartial, to ignore them is folly. For instance, the human body needs periodic rest, and when we consistently ignore that basic need, we cannot function at an optimum level. If we choose to ignore the laws of nutrition by living mainly on junk food and carbonated soft drinks, eventually we pay a price. Does this mean, then, that we have no choice but to obey those laws or risk suffering adverse consequences? The above verse suggests that the spiritual aspirant somehow emerges victorious over nature. If this is the case, our next question should be, "How is that possible?" An aphoristic remark by Francis Bacon provides a clue: "We cannot command nature except by obeying her."[16] So, what exactly does that mean?

Imagine a young athlete who is training to become a tightrope walker: first, he practices from only a few feet above the ground, then somewhat higher, but using a safety net. Week after week, he falls and falls but still keeps on trying, going higher and higher. This is what Philippe Petit did until he was confident and skillful enough to walk a wire strung between the Twin Towers of the World Trade Center in 1974. As a novice, he had no choice but to obey the law of gravity; but as an accomplished high-wire artist, he "conquered" gravity by obeying another law—the law of equilibrium. A quote from John Stuart Mill explains:

> Though we cannot emancipate ourselves from the laws of nature as a whole, we can escape from any particular law of nature, if we are able to withdraw ourselves from the circumstances in which it acts. Though we can do nothing except through laws of nature, we can use one law to counteract another.[17]

Let us take another verse from *The Voice of the Silence*: "Give up thy life, if thou would'st live" (vs. 21). As in Matthew 16:25, we are told to give up something that is deeply ingrained in us—our sense of a personal self—so deeply embedded that we might consider it to be a law of nature. At the early stages of growth, this is absolutely necessary. A child grows by taking in all sorts of experiences and knowledge, developing various skills and abilities in the process. This process of accumulation, which is centered around the personal self, may be compared to the law of addition. Later, when the child becomes an adult and realizes its connections and responsibilities to others, a change takes place, which by analogy resembles the law of subtraction. In the spiritual life this translates to letting go of selfish attachments, rigid modes of thought, personal ambition, resentments and biases, all of which helps to clear the way for the finer and nobler impulses characteristic of our higher nature. In simplistic terms, we go from a mode of taking to one of giving, and the result is a voluntary reciprocity that is beneficial to all.

Nature, Part 4

Help nature and work on with her . . . (vs. 66)

As human beings, endowed with the faculty of thought and the ability to make choices, how are we to view our relationship with nature? Western science has taken the approach of observing and investigating nature (*naturam observare*), resulting in amazing discoveries and technological advances. Another school of thought urges us to follow nature (*naturam sequi*), the implication being that nature serves as an exemplar of moral principles. The latter view is expressed in this passage by Alexander Pope:

> First follow *Nature,* and your judgment frame
> By her just standard, which is still the same:
> Unerring Nature, still divinely bright,
> One clear, unchang'd, and universal light,
> Life, force, and beauty, must to all impart,
> At once the source, and end, and test of art.[18]

A contrarian view is encapsulated in Tennyson's oft-quoted phrase "Nature, red in tooth and claw," a graphic depiction of predatory violence occurring daily in the natural world. To those who hold nature as a moral beacon for humanity, John Stuart Mill would argue:

> The order of nature, in so far as unmodified by man, is such as no being, whose attributes are justice and benevolence, would have made with the intention that his rational creatures should follow it as an example. . . . In sober truth, nearly all the things which men are hanged or imprisoned for doing to one another are nature's every-day performances.[19]

The raw forces of nature have wreaked death, destruction, and misery on a scale of epic proportions, accomplishing this by means of droughts and pestilence, fire and floods, tsunamis and earthquakes, cyclones and tornados, extreme heat and bone-numbing cold—all deadly weapons that have destroyed property, lives, and entire cities.

So, who is correct, Pope or Mill? An unbridgeable chasm seems to separate their views. Perhaps they are both right, depending on the definition of nature being used. If I may borrow the words of H. P. Blavatsky, one is thinking of the "eternal and uncreate nature," whereas the other is looking only at the "flitting shadows and finite unrealities."[20]

Nature, Part 5

Help nature and work on with her; and nature will regard thee as one of her creators and make obeisance (vs. 66).

What does it mean to help nature, to collaborate with her? This verse calls for careful consideration. Western science speaks of "conquering" the forces of nature. In actual fact, nobody conquers (i.e., defeats) the forces of nature, but one natural law can be used to neutralize the effects of another. Jet planes overcome the force of gravity through the power of jet propulsion, but the law of gravity remains as unapologetic and operational as ever.

The Russian novelist Ivan Turgenev observed that "nature is not a temple, but a workshop, and man's the workman in it."[21] Two notable examples of working with the physical side of nature come to mind. Luther Burbank created over eight hundred strains and varieties of plants by working *with,* not *against,* nature. John Roebling designed and oversaw the construction of the Brooklyn Bridge—then the world's longest suspension bridge—not by *defeating* the laws of nature, but by working *with* them. Turgenev's view seems to comport well with the Russian occultist Helena Petrovna Blavatsky statement in *The Secret Doctrine* that humanity cannot "get rid of the burden of its co-operative work with nature" (2:446). But was she referring to the material side of nature, the life behind the outer forms, or both?

The above citation from the *Voice* is followed by another, which says when we become cocreators with nature, she will open "the portals of her secret chambers [and] lay bare . . . the treasures hidden in the very depths of her pure virgin bosom" (vs. 67). So where exactly are those secret chambers? Do they even exist? Aren't they nothing more than figurative language and poetic fancy? In his commentary, N. Sri Ram suggests that the secret chambers "are not something mysterious in some far-away heaven; they are everywhere—in every tree and rock, in the sky and in the earth, in all the creatures that inhabit them."[22] If we want to find out the truth for ourselves, we might follow the advice of the mystic Flower Newhouse:

> Prepare yourself for encounters with nature by being quiet and listening with keen perceptiveness. You need to walk alone to behold, to think, to feel, to be instructed. Be reverent, be appreciative, be perceptive. Watch the horizons. All of a sudden, everything will change, and you will find yourself stilled in wonder. You will be so at one with the intelligence of nature that from your encounter will come a shower of inflowing power, the like of which you have never before received.[23]

Has Patience Become an Anachronism?

Have patience, candidate, as one who fears no failure,
courts no success (vs. 137).

Patience has long been recognized as a virtue, but in today's fast-paced digital world of instant everything, it seems to be viewed by some as a quaint throwback to a slower, predigital era. Worse still, others consider it an obstacle to their restless pursuit of personal ambition. On the other hand, there may be a few who, lacking dreams and motivation, cloak their slothful state with the respectable robes of patience and prudence.

Many traditional ways of doing things have been washed away by the powerful digital tsunami, but we can rest assured that patience is still a sine qua non of the spiritual life. It is mentioned more than once in the Mahatma Letters. In a letter to A.P. Sinnett from one of the

Adepts, Sinnett is reminded that "[the] great man is he who is strongest in the exercise of patience."[24] Anyone who has embarked upon the path of self-transformation knows that it is not the journey of a single day. Patience and fortitude are indispensable elements in that process.

When we are very young, our patience is a finite resource. To a young girl, the three-hour drive to grandma's house may seem unbearable, but by the time she graduates from high school, the thought of four years at a university seems quite manageable. In this sense, patience has a quantitative aspect—it grows. As adults, we have more patience than we did as children. Also, some people have more of it than others. This may or may not be a good thing. If the house you are in is going up in flames, it may not be the best moment to display stoic patience. With respect to Proverbs 19:2, haste does not always make waste.

So we learn to bide our time while working towards a goal or waiting for an expected outcome, whether it is learning to play the piano or waiting for the waitress in a crowded restaurant to bring us a menu. By comparison, the patience of the spiritual disciple has a distinct *qualitative* difference; it is not based on results or reward or personal satisfaction. It arises from a sublime detachment that allows one to do the right thing *because* it is the right thing to do. The Bhagavad Gita agrees: "Without concern for results, perform the necessary action."[25] As aspirants on the spiritual path, we may or may not see our efforts come to fruition, but it really doesn't matter. We do the right thing and leave the outcome to Karma.

Don't Think! Just Do It!

KSHANTI, patience sweet, that nought can ruffle (vs. 209).

Early in the third fragment of *The Voice of the Silence*, we are introduced to the six paramitas, those golden keys which unlock the portals to the other shore. Mahayana Buddhists also refer to them as the Six Perfections, one of which is *kshanti*, whose meaning includes not only patience but forbearance, tolerance, endurance, and acceptance. To explore the distinctions among these nuances of meaning would require more discussion than space permits, so what follows are a few random musings.

We live in a time when worldly conditions are not conducive to the cultivation of patience. On all sides we are beleaguered by calls to act—and to act quickly—whether it pertains to advancing one's career, solving the world's problems, or finding enlightenment. There is a tacit assumption that those who practice patience will be left behind, an opinion perhaps best expressed by the Nike trademark, JUST DO IT. Those enamored by the Gospel of Instant Gratification are likely to dismiss statements such as this one from Bishop Joseph Hall (1574–1656): "Perfection is the child of Time";[26] or this from *The Voice of the Silence*: "Long and weary is the way before thee" (vs 74). *Do it and do it now* is the siren call of the day.

The annals of history record numerous examples of powerful, self-driven individuals who ruthlessly pursued their personal ambitions, seemingly without a moment's pause for quiet introspection. When he died at the age of thirty-two, Alexander the Great had conquered virtually the entire known world, an empire stretching from Macedonia to India. Five centuries later, Flavius Arrianus Xenophon, a student of Epictetus, wrote, "The splendid achievements of Alexander are the clearest possible proof that neither strength of body, nor noble blood, nor success in war . . . can make a man happy, unless he can win one more victory in addition to those the world thinks great—the victory over himself."[27]

So how does one develop kshanti, a perfection easier to conceive in the abstract than to realize in daily life? The prayer of St. Teresa of Avila advises us to proceed this way:

> Let nothing disturb you,
> Let nothing frighten you,
> All things are passing away.
> God never changes.
> Patience obtains all things.[28]

Others find it through a reverential intimacy with nature. In her book *Dakota—A Spiritual Geography,* Kathleen Norris describes this alchemical process: "The silence of the Plains, this great un-peopled landscape of earth and sky, is much like the silence one finds in a monastery, an unfathomable silence that has the power to re-form you."[29]

Prolonged contemplation of God, either in its transcendent aspect or as it manifests through nature, is a powerful palliative for those afflicted by impatience.

Poets Should Be Grateful

Step out from sunlight into shade,
to make more room for others (vs. 140).

An old Jewish prayer praises the Lord for having made a distinction between light and darkness. Poets should be thankful, too, for they often utilize those images in their craft. The contrast between light and darkness is rich in symbolism, one instance of which is found in this popular invocation from the Upanishads: "From darkness, lead me to Light."[30] William Blake employs the same symbolism in his poem "Auguries of Innocence": "God is Light to those poor souls who dwell in night." Moreover, the symmetry of the Latin phrase *Lux et Veritas* (Light and Truth) is so self-evident that Yale University adopted it as its motto.

So, in the face of all this, why in the passage from the *Voice* cited above is the disciple being asked to step out of the sunlight and move into the shadows? Does not light symbolize the Platonic ideals of goodness, truth, and beauty? Are we to believe that life is a zero-sum game in which goodness is a finite resource and therefore to be distributed on a time-share basis? The key to this enigma lies in understanding the style in which *The Voice of the Silence* was written.

Virtually its every page features lines of exquisite poetic imagery. The motif of light appears again and again, yet in differing contexts. Verse 80 describes the "unfading golden light of Spirit," while verse 34 issues a warning about a certain type of light that bewitches the senses and blinds the mind. Verse 28 advises the disciple not to mistake the fires of passion "for the sunlight of life," while verse 14 equates "bathing in the sunlight of thy life" as being a problem. Again, what are we to make of all this? It seems confusing.

The language of poetry is pliable, flexible, and elastic. We do not read poetry with the mindset of an attorney or accountant. Regarding the citation at the top of this essay, could the words *sunlight* and *shade* hold a psychological meaning? Let's say that *sunlight* represents the ego's desire to bask in the spotlight and be the center of attention. Let's say that *shade* represents the attitude of one who is seeking neither attention nor recognition but simply doing good work for the sake of the work. In the eyes of the world, that person may appear to be insignificant, because people usually crave the spotlight for purposes of self-aggrandizement. But as Leadbeater noted, "The only power which the disciple should desire is that which makes him seem as nothing in the eyes of others."[31]

The Nuances of Light and Darkness

This earth . . . is but the dismal entrance leading to the twilight that precedes the valley of true light (vs. 18).

Blavatsky's metaphoric use of light in *The Voice of the Silence* is delightfully unconventional. In verse 140, the aspirant is told to "step out from sunlight into shade," but in verse 18 (cited above) the implication is that he should be moving out of darkness and into light. It is the same metaphor used to very different effect, a literary distinction that serves to enrich the esthetic enjoyment of the reader. Also surprising is the metaphorical pairing of the words *light* with *valley*. Symbolically, valleys are often used to represent pain and suffering (the valley of the shadow of death), whereas mountains suggest triumph, illumination, or a wider perspective. Again, in verse 37 Blavatsky refers to the "Vale of Bliss" rather than associating a transcendent state of consciousness with a mountain peak. But this is not without precedent. Consider this passage from the *Tao Te Ching*: "The Valley Spirit never dies. . . . [It] is the base from which Heaven and Earth sprang. It is there within us all the while." Authors have on occasion used valleys to symbolize safety, growth, warmth, fertility, and abundance.

Shifting from style to substance, let us note that some readers may recoil at the depiction of earthly life as being dismal. Yet one cannot deny the existence of suffering. Human existence involves an oscillation of peaks and valleys, pleasure and pain, weal and woe. While the suffering often cuts deeply, the moments of felicity and mirth are all too ephemeral. Having observed this sad state of affairs, Fyodor Dostoevsky allegedly confessed, "There is only one thing that I dread: not to be worthy of my sufferings."[32]

We do not always listen to our better angels. We see through a glass darkly. Aspiring to higher things, we quickly tire and succumb to the gravitational pull of personal desires. Yet if we struggle, it is because we are human. I am reminded of a quote attributed to Somerset Maugham: "Only a mediocre person is always at his best."[33] We will fall, but we get up again. To err is human, but to get up in the face of adversity is heroic. The journey from darkness through twilight to the true light is the one true journey, a journey of many lifetimes. Patience and devotion are our companions. If fears and doubts arise, we have the testimony of countless shamans and saints and sages affirming that it can be done. Faith and fortitude, too, are our companions. Follow the true light, dimly perceived at first, like the partial sunlight seen from the bottom of a well; but as we continue to put one step in front of the other its growing intensity and brilliance will erase these pervasive shadows that we now take for light.

Beauty vs. Glamour

*Beware, lest dazzled by illusive radiance thy soul should linger
and be caught in its deceptive light* (vs. 33).

Here's a simple exercise. Take a sheet of paper and draw a line straight down the middle. In the first column make a list of things you consider to be beautiful. In the second column list those things that you consider to be glamourous. As a guideline, let us suggest that true beauty loses none of its charm over time; and glamour, which at first appears exciting and novel, eventually reveals itself to be superficial and hollow. So here is the question. If you had made this list ten or twenty years ago, would your answers have been the same? Would some items now in the second column have appeared then in the first? And if this is the case, how do you account for your change of perspective?

The above verse sounds a cautionary note regarding the Hall of Learning, a metaphor in the *Voice* used to designate a certain stage of growth. Here aspirants learn—among other things—to gain self-control over their desire nature. As Annie Besant observed, emotions and feelings are powerful forces in the lives of virtually every human being:

> The life of sensation is the greater part of the life of the majority.
> For those below the average, this life of sensation is the whole life.
> For a few advanced beings this life of sensation is transcended.

The vast majority occupy the various stages which stretch between the life of sensation and that which has transcended such sensation: stages of mixed sensation, emotion and thought in diverse proportions.[34]

Few individuals are capable of living a life without being swayed by the pleasure-seeking principle. Those on the spiritual path have graduated from that sector of humanity where pleasing sensations are the end-all and be-all of existence. They find themselves in an intermediary state, aspiring to lofty and selfless goals but still susceptible to the temptations of sensual pleasures and personal vanities. What is needed at this stage is the sword of spiritual discrimination, *viveka*, about which Krishnamurti speaks in chapter one of *At the Feet of the Master*. Unlike a sword of steel whose blade dulls with repeated use, the sword of discriminative wisdom is honed to a razor-sharp edge when consistently applied as a means of severing our emotional bonds from the deceptive lure of shallow and short-lived attractions.

Cultivating Divine Indifference

Thy Soul-gaze center on the One Pure Light,
the Light that is free from affection (vs. 255).

What is the nature of this light that stands in relation to the aspirant as a cynosure? How is it that a book advocating compassion also instructs the disciple to embrace a lodestar whose defining feature is the absence of affection? We know that purity is recognized in many traditions as a prerequisite to spiritual advancement, but what exactly is the problem with affection? Is there not a contradiction here?

The incongruity resolves itself if one views the word *affection* as a proxy for feelings in general, which at the most basic level are experienced as pleasure or pain. Some people are so strongly swayed by attraction and repulsion that they allow these feelings to define their sense of who they are. It is for the purpose of emancipating oneself from these emotional tethers that aspirants are urged to practice vairāgya. *Vairāgya* has been defined as "desirelessness," a term that to the uninitiated may suggest a lethargic individual completely lacking in drive and initiative. Such a characterization is totally off the mark. As remarked above, Clara Codd defines *vairāgya* as "divine indifference . . . the ability to stand serene and steady under all circumstances."[35] *The Voice of the Silence* describes it as becoming "indifferent to objects of perception" (vs .3), which we should note is not the same as becoming oblivious. A psychologist cannot effectively treat a client if she allows herself to identify with her patient's maladies. A pastor cannot comfort a grieving widow if he, too, succumbs to her understandable feelings of grief.

In the beginning stages of the path, the practice of vairāgya is best applied to the small things of daily life. Being aware of how we judge other people through our prism of likes and dislikes is a good place to start. Observing how easily and imperceptibly our actions are influenced by the pleasure-seeking principle, instead of by high and lofty aspirations, is another. It is not easy, it is not quick, but with persistent effort progress can be made. Yet when, after a period of due diligence, signs of progress emerge, the disciple should be wary of becoming complacent. The human mind has been compared to a garden, and any gardener knows that seeds from last season's weeds may lie buried in the soil.

Giving without Taking

Give light to all, but take from none (vs. 291).

The advice offered by religious scriptures on how a human being should act in the world usually falls into two broad categories:

thoughts and behaviors that should be avoided or minimized, and those that should be developed and strengthened. For one of many examples, we might turn to the second chapter of Patanjali's *Yoga Sutras*, where we find a short list of restraints (*yamas*) followed by another short list of observances (*niyamas*). Generally speaking, all such moral guidelines address what traditionally have been referred to as *virtues* and *vices*, the idea being to cultivate the former and weed out the latter. It is not uncommon to find discussions of one leading to discussions of the other. We see an instance of this coupling within the following aphorism: "Give light to all, but take from none." While it is readily apparent that the first half of this binary dictum refers to virtuous behavior and the second to actions considered undesirable, the interpretation and implementation of it may not be so obvious.

Some Theosophists may take "Give light to all" as an inference to share their esoteric knowledge, gained over years of study. While we do not promote proselytizing, some erudite polyhistor is sure to quote the maxim of Thucydides, "To know a thing and not to express it, is all one as if he knew it not."[36] But in short order, another member will issue a rejoinder by citing Lao Tsu, "Those who know do not talk. Those who talk do not know."[37] You can imagine the interesting discussion that ensues from such a juxtaposition of ideas.

The moral stricture to "take from none" may be seen as a condensation of an earlier verse from *The Voice of the Silence:* "Step out from sunlight into shade, to make more room for others" (vs. 140). It addresses the subtle—and sometimes not too subtle—tendency of craving attention, of seeking the limelight. All such tendencies are impediments on the path, and shifting our attention to others and finding ways to alleviate their suffering is the best antidote to self-centered habituations.

Cardinal Newman once wrote: "[A gentleman] is seldom prominent in conversation, and never wearisome. He makes light of favors while he does them, and seems to be receiving when he is conferring. He never speaks of himself except when compelled."[38] That is exceptionally good advice, although not so easy to follow.

No Compliments, Please! I'm Feigning Humility

Shun praise, O devotee.
Praise leads to self-delusion (vs. 117).

While we can all agree that self-delusion is never a good thing, can we say the same of praise? Consider this: whether praise is beneficial or detrimental depends entirely on the circumstances. I think most of us understand that excessive praise can lead to self-delusion, self-absorption, poor judgement, reckless and irresponsible behavior, an exaggerated sense of one's abilities, and even arrogance and contempt. But when warranted, and in moderation, praise can be a good thing. What parents would not commend their child for improving her grades in school? Who would not congratulate a friend for completing his first marathon? Who would fault a concert audience for a spirited standing ovation given to a world-class orchestra, following a bravura performance? As an honest and spontaneous expression of respect, appreciation, or love, the value of praise is not to be overlooked. As a tool for molding and shaping desirable behavior, it has proven to be quite effective, provided it has not been distributed in a profligate and indiscriminate manner.

The maxim from the *Voice* that opens this essay tells us to shun praise, but suppose we are on the receiving end of a compliment. As aspirants, how are we to react? Oddly enough, there are some who assume that "becoming spiritual" means abandoning common sense. Nothing could be further from the truth. It is best to follow the social norms of good behavior by accepting compliments graciously and with a measure of modesty. Yet some people have difficulty with this. When complimented on what appears to be a new jacket, they cavalierly say, "Oh, no, this is nothing special—just a used jacket I picked up at a rummage sale." Such a response is insensitive because it ignores a gesture of goodwill; it may even appear insulting. A shorter and more appropriate response would be, "Why, thank you. I'm glad you like it." Rebuffing an honest compliment is not evidence of modesty or spirituality, but rather an indication that one is lacking in good manners. Another example might be the recognition a manager receives from bringing a project to successful fruition. The magnanimous response would be something like, "Thank you, but I had lots of help from a great team of people. They deserve most of the credit." Aspirants do not solicit praise from others, but they graciously accept it when given, without making a habit of marinating in it.

Elevate Your Mind, Not Your Ego

Self-gratulation, O disciple, is like unto a lofty tower,
up which a haughty fool has climbed. Theron he sits in
prideful solitude and unperceived by any but himself (vs. 118).

One of the distinctive features of *The Voice of the Silence* is how it strikes a judicious balance between words of encouragement and notes of caution. Passages like "each sincere attempt wins its reward in time" (vs. 274) are counterbalanced by verses such as "long and weary is the way before thee" (vs. 74). Some readers find the latter type to be off-putting, but I am reminded of the principle of truth in advertising. Treading the spiritual path is not a casual walk in the park on a warm Sunday afternoon but rather a long and arduous and sometimes lonely journey on a road filled with potholes, detours, and potential dangers, as well as the sublime joys that one might expect. Yet there is no shortage of *faux* gurus who prefer to sugarcoat the entire undertaking, and their one-sided portrayal has an obvious appeal to those lacking in discernment. It is to its credit that the *Voice* gives a more balanced and realistic approach, one that is inspirational as well as cautionary, idealistic as well as realistic.

Many of the pitfalls that the aspirant will face are mentioned, including those of ignorance, attachment, fear, illusion, and impurity, to name just a few. Some are emphasized in dramatic fashion, while others are alluded to or only mentioned in passing. Why is this? Why are they not put forth in systematic fashion? The answer is simple. It is because this is a poetic work and not a scholarly treatise, in contrast to Thomas Aquinas' *Summa Theologica* or Aristotle's *Nicomachean Ethics*. Instead of employing learned expositions on the nature of virtue and vice, the *Voice* makes use of vivid poetic imagery to drive home its message. The simile in the above citation is a case in point: what better image of pride than that of a conceited fool dwelling alone in his imaginary tower supported only by an inflated sense of self-esteem and a surfeit of self-adulation?

The fact that pride is universally recognized as an impediment to spirituality shows how pervasive it is. We are not immune. Even when the worldly manifestations of pride have been done away with, it often emerges in the form of spiritual pride. We might remember the words of C. S. Lewis: "A proud man is always looking down on things and people; and, of course, as long as you are looking down, you cannot see something that is above you."[39]

Doctrinal Didactics

Learn above all to separate head-learning from Soul-Wisdom,
the 'Eye' from the 'Heart' Doctrine (vs. 111).

Several verses in the second fragment of the *Voice* refer to the doctrines of the "Eye" and the "Heart." Since this book is Mme.

Blavatsky's translation of a Buddhist text dating back millennia, is it possible that the word *doctrine* meant something different then than it does today? In current usage it may refer to a specific governmental policy, especially in foreign affairs, e.g., the Truman Doctrine or the Reagan Doctrine. It can also refer to a comprehensive body of knowledge taught by qualified instructors, as in the case of economic doctrine, Catholic doctrine, or military doctrine. Sometimes it has a narrower focus, as when the term is used to identify a specific tenet of a religion or philosophy: Roman Catholics speak of vicarious atonement; Protestants speak of *sola fide* (faith alone); and students of Theosophy speak of unity, emanation, periodicity, and Karma. In short, the word *doctrine* may refer either to *an entire body of teachings* or to *a single principle* within those teachings.

Yet another example of doctrine is a theory that has been developed over time through debate and critical analysis. For example, in American political discourse, the doctrine of states' rights was first put forth in the Federalist Papers and later codified as the Tenth Amendment of the US Constitution.

Within the Christian tradition we find the Just War Doctrine, first articulated by St. Augustine and later developed more fully by Thomas Aquinas. Still another example is the Buddhist doctrine of impermanence, a core principle that has been shaped and refined over time by generations of scholars.

To summarize, modern definitions of the word *doctrine* include (1) a policy of state, (2) a body of teachings, (3) a principle or tenet, and (4) a theory supported by evidence and formulated over time. Returning to the question posed earlier, which of these definitions of doctrine best describes how it is used in *The Voice of the Silence?* Clearly, we can rule out the first definition, but what about the others? Students are encouraged to read the text and draw their own conclusions. More remains to be said, and we will continue our discussion in the next essay.

Doctrinal Dilation

The 'Doctrine of the Eye' is for the crowd,
the 'Doctrine of the Heart,' for the elect (vs. 119).

In the above verse, *eye* and *heart* are code words for *exoteric* and
esoteric. Mme. Blavatsky states as much in a short gloss. Dilat-
ing further in *The Secret Doctrine,* she says: "Unable to teach *all*
that had been imparted to him—owing to his pledges—though he
taught a philosophy built upon the groundwork of the true esoteric
knowledge, the Buddha gave to the world only its *outward* material
body and kept its *soul* for his Elect" (1:xxi).

The idea of esoteric teachings is not new to students of Theosophy; and who is not familiar with this verse from the Gospel of
Matthew (7:6): "Give not that which is holy unto the dogs, neither
cast your pearls before the swine, lest haply they trample them
under their feet, and turn and rend you." There has always been
one set of teachings for the multitudes and another for chelas and
disciples, as was the case in the mystery schools of ancient Greece
and Egypt. According to G. de Purucker,

> [They] formed the inner focus of the ancient thought, and the
> doctrines there studied were called the 'Heart-Doctrine,' because
> they represented the doctrines that were hid; and the various
> philosophies that they expounded in public were called the 'Eye-
> Doctrine,' because they were doctrines in exoteric phrasing of the
> things that were seen and not the things that were hid. The Heart-
> Doctrine comprised the solutions of the enigmas of being, and
> these solutions were put forth in exoteric form under the guise
> of allegory and in mythological treatment, and formed the Eye-
> Doctrine, or the exoteric religions or philosophies.[40]

After hearing of the existence of esoteric knowledge, some wonder how to access it. Well, it is not something that can be looked
up in an encyclopedia or discovered in the manner of a cryptana-

lyst deciphering enemy code, as did Alan Turing for the British in World War II. True esoteric knowledge is not so easily won. Aldous Huxley said it well: "Knowledge is a function of being. When there is a change in the being of the knower, there is a corresponding change in the nature and amount of knowing."[41] In other words, curiosity is not enough; intellectual brilliance is not enough; even a dogged determination is not enough, so long as the seeker has not undergone an inner transformation.

Thus I Have Heard

The first repeat in pride: "Behold, I know";
the last, they who in humbleness have garnered, low confess,
"Thus I have heard" (vs. 119).

There is a reason why lecturers for the Theosophical Society are not introduced as experts. In other contexts it may be appropriate, provided the speaker has the necessary credentials, whether they be in the field of early Florentine architecture, the latest research on heart disease, the music of the Baroque period, or the latest methodology in DNA testing. These types of knowledge are observable, demonstrable, empirical, quantifiable. Furthermore, if you have the interest, the aptitude, and the ambition, you could become an expert in an area of specialized knowledge. We respect experts. We depend on them in our daily life. When you inform a mechanic that your automobile engine is knocking, you expect him to inspect the engine and say something like, "I know what it is, and I know how to fix it." If instead he says, "Well, I've heard that it might be the timing belt, or maybe a worn cylinder wall," that is your cue to say, "Thanks for your time," and go to another mechanic.

The difficult questions of religion and philosophy are not to be resolved in the laboratory or by statistical analysis. Faith is an indispensable element of religion. Philosophical debates involve speculation, and they often span centuries. Therefore, when Theosophists deliver lectures on topics with some degree of sublimity, they generally adopt the attitude of "Thus I have heard" rather than "Listen to me, I know." This stance is very different from the posture taken by those who know very little but seem quite certain about the ultimate truth of things. As seekers of truth, what have we really garnered from our seeking? If it is only head learning, it has limited utility. "All that we have heard about God, the Spirit, Atman, the Void," says Sri Madhava Ashish, "derives at its best from other people's experience. . . . It may be their knowledge, but it is not ours; and that is why we are still seekers and not finders."[42]

So if you tell me that your understanding of a religious or philosophical matter is rock solid; if you claim to have read all there is to read on the matter; if you feel that your knowledge is complete and unassailable; if you are absolutely certain of all this, you might consider the therapeutic remedy of standing before a mirror and saying, "I may be wrong. I may be profoundly wrong. I may be desperately, irreparably wrong." And in doing so, chances are that you may be right.

O, Ignorant Disciple

But even ignorance is better than head-learning with
no Soul-Wisdom to illuminate and guide it (vs. 113).

Although compassion is the predominant theme of *The Voice of the Silence*, ignorance holds the distinction of being mentioned at the very onset: "These instructions are for those ignorant of the dangers of the lower IDDHI" (vs. 1). All the other motifs—the Three Halls, the Two Paths, the Seven Portals, etc.—serve only to help the aspirant become the type of human being who not only *feels* compassion but also *acts* from it. Yet before the aspirant can initiate this transformation, he must recognize and deal with his own ignorance. Here, ignorance is not obtuseness or hebetude, but *nescience*: lack of awareness, or being uninformed. That this is a matter of some urgency is evidenced by the fact that over a dozen verses refer to ignorance, either explicitly or implicitly. That may not seem like a huge number, but in a small book of just over three hundred verses, it is more than enough to make the point: ignorance is an obstacle to spiritual growth. Not surprisingly, Buddhists list it as the first of the Twelve Nidanas.[43]

While you may recall that the *Voice* is cast as a conversation between a guru and his disciple, fragment 1 is more akin to a monologue in which the disciple listens quietly, perhaps in tacit recognition of his ignorance. In verse 18, the guru addresses his protégé as "O ignorant disciple," a salutation that really means, "You who have much to learn." In verse 24 the disciple learns of the Hall of Ignorance, a metaphor for the preliminary stage of the path, wherein he is advised not to conflate human passions with "the sunlight of life" (vs. 28) or to succumb to the false allure of earthly illusions (vss. 33–35). The development of this theme is facilitated by some of the most exquisite poetic imagery imaginable, as in verse 112, where a soul encumbered by ignorance is likened to a mute songbird confined within a cage. The reader may sense the repetition of this motif slowly building to a climax, somewhat like the gradual snare drum crescendo in Ravel's "Bolero." Yet when the climax arrives (vs. 113), it does so with an unexpected twist, abruptly depicting ignorance as the *lesser* of two evils. If faced with the possibility of misusing his knowledge so that others will come to harm, it is preferable for the aspirant to remain in a state of relative ignorance until he has developed the necessary power of discernment. The spirit of *ahimsa* (Skt., "do no harm") trumps the desire to know, especially when that thirst for knowledge is driven by short-sighted and self-serving considerations.

The Human Condition

Behold the hosts of souls.
Watch how they hover o'er the stormy sea of human life,
and how, exhausted, bleeding, broken-winged,
they drop one after another on the swelling waves (vs. 36).

The first of the Four Noble Truths of Siddhartha Gautama recognizes the existence and pervasiveness of suffering. Verse 36 of *The Voice of the Silence* is a powerful dramatization of that truth. Any sober assessment of the "human condition," a phrase that gained currency following the 1933 publication of Andre Malraux's *La Condition Humaine (Man's Fate)* recognizes that suffering is concomitant with living. HPB's graphic depiction of human suffering over the turbulent sea of life provides us with an image whose vividness is almost palpable. Gustave Doré, the French artist who created the unforgettable illustrations for Dante's *Inferno* and Milton's *Paradise Lost,* would have been artistically inspired by this passage. But the same verse may strike others as over-the-top melodrama born of overwrought Victorian sensibilities. They may prefer this gentler, subdued description of the human condition by Shelley in his poem entitled "Time":

> Ocean of Time, whose waters of deep woe
> Are brackish with the salt of human tears!

Those lines are very nice and concise, but for some people they may lack power and intensity.

Another survey of the human condition appears in an epistle by St. Cyprian, a Christian theologian of the third century:

For a brief space conceive yourself to be transported to one of the loftiest peaks of some inaccessible mountain, thence gaze on the appearances of things lying below you, and with eyes turned in various directions look upon the eddies of the billowy world, while you yourself are removed from earthly contacts—you will at once begin to feel compassion for the world.[44]

I believe this is the intended effect of verse 36—to arouse compassion for those who suffer. It was compassion, after all, which prompted Master K. H., in one of his letters to Sinnett, to utter the words, "Poor, poor humanity!"[45]

Dwell on this sad state of affairs too long and you may feel a bit bewildered. These are not pleasant facts, but they are facts; which is why the disciple is told that if he reacts to the roaring turmoil of the world in the manner of a frightened turtle retreating within the relative safety of his carapace, he is not yet ready to enter the field of battle (vs. 15). Fortunately, we grow through successive incarnations, learning from our mistakes and, in the words of Milton, gaining "knowledge of good bought dear by knowing ill."[46]

Fail Today, Succeed Tomorrow

Learn that no efforts, not the smallest—whether in the right or wrong direction—can vanish from the world of causes (vs. 147).

The above verse obviously refers to Karma, "that unseen and unknown law. . . . *which adjusts wisely, intelligently and equitably* each effect to its cause, tracing the latter back to its producer."[47] Karma is mentioned several times in the *Voice*, and verses such as the cited one have both a reassuring and a premonitory quality: *reassuring* in the sense that the disciple knows his efforts will bear fruit, but *premonitory* in that his misdeeds will also bear fruit. Karma has been described as that "unerring law which adjusts cause to effect, on the physical, mental and spiritual planes."[48] Harsh words and selfish actions bear their fruit, just as surely as do those motivated by kindness and altruism. As a wise teacher once told his chela, "Life and the struggle for Adeptship would be too easy, had we all scavengers behind us to sweep away the *effects* we have generated through our own rashness and presumption."[49]

Knowledge of Karma allows the disciple to persevere "as one who doth for evermore endure." He is not discouraged by setbacks and obstacles. He knows that he is engaged in a work of many lifetimes and that causes set in motion do not always reach a resolution within one lifetime. The process of self-transformation is an example. The disciple struggles to develop qualities in which he may be lacking, such as patience or tolerance. It is slow, painstaking work. And even when success seems to have been achieved, it pays to be vigilant. In the words of Francis Bacon, "Let not a man trust his victory over his nature too far; for nature will lay buried a great time, and yet revive upon the occasion or temptation."[50]

Karma also creates opportunities (or a lack of them). It is said that those disciples who make the most of their present opportunities will have even greater opportunities for service in the future. Conversely, those who fail to take advantage of existing opportunities will find them scarce or nonexistent in their next incarnation. You may recall the parable of the talents, in which three servants were given money to invest while their master traveled abroad. When the master returned, the two servants who invested wisely were rewarded, but the third who did nothing out of fear was rebuked. We need not be afraid of failure in this business of discipleship. As long as we persevere, all setbacks are temporary. As HPB said, "For those who win onwards there is reward past all telling—the power to bless and save humanity; for those who fail, there are other lives in which success may come."[51]

A Special Form of Service

Give light and comfort to the toiling pilgrim,
and seek out him who knows still less than thou (vs. 158).

I am proud to say that there are many members of the Theosophical Society who devote part of their time and money to doing philanthropic work. This is commendable, because every effort along these lines helps to make a difference. There is, however, another form of service that only a Theosophist can deliver, and by that I mean a person who studies Theosophy and strives to make it a part of his or her life. In section 12 of *The Key to Theosophy*, Blavatsky describes the type of service Theosophists should perform: "We believe in relieving the starvation of the Soul, as much, if not more, than the emptiness of the stomach."[52]

The truths of Theosophy have the power to change people's lives, but some Theosophists demur at the thought of teaching others, perhaps out of modesty, shyness, or lack of confidence. To these gentle souls, the *Voice* says, "Seek out him who knows still less than thou" (vs. 158). On the other hand, some members seem to care only about their own intellectual development. To these savants, the *Voice* has a short but stern admonishment: "The selfish devotee lives to no purpose" (vs. 153). Similarly, in one of the Mahatma Letters a self-absorbed chela is told that "the chief object of the T.S. is not so much to gratify individual aspirations as to serve our fellow men."[53] Speaking to members of the Theosophical Society, Blavatsky emphasized that we have a duty to be of service, particularly "to all those who are poorer and more helpless than we are ourselves."[54] If we fail in our duty, it becomes a debt that "leaves us spiritually insolvent and moral bankrupts in our next incarnation."[55] Finally, there are those devotees, few in number, fortunately, who consider themselves exempt from humanitarian service, since they fancy themselves as serving the Christ, the Buddha, or the Masters—and what is more important: serving soup or higher beings? Confucius had a tart response for this group: "You are not able even to serve man. How can you serve the spirits?"[56]

What it all boils down to is this: there really is no good excuse for a Theosophist not to be of service. C. Jinarajadasa, a former president of the Theosophical Society, summed it up admirably:

If each member . . . will keep in mind that he is a member in order
to call out the Hidden Light in all his fellow men, he will not only
strengthen his Society, but find that there is born within him greater
strength to bear the difficulties of his own Karma, as also fuller Light
to see the way towards the unfoldment of the Godhead within him.[57]

The Arduous Vertical Ascent

The Path is one for all; the means to reach the goal
must vary with the pilgrims (vs. 197).

In her book *From the Outer Court to the Inner Sanctum*, Annie
Besant provides a visual image symbolizing the long, arduous process of human evolution:

> I see a great mountain standing in space, with a road that winds
> round the mountain, round and round until the summit is
> reached. . . . As we trace the road upwards along this spiral track,
> we see how it ends at the summit of the mountain—that it leads
> to a mighty Temple, a Temple as of white marble, radiant, which
> stands there shining out against the ethereal blue. That Temple is
> the goal of the pilgrimage, and they who are in it . . . remain there
> only for the helping of those who are still climbing.[58]

The mass of humanity is traversing this protracted, circuitous road,
unaware that it extends beyond the span of a single lifetime. They live
in what *The Voice of Silence* dubs the Hall of Sorrow, hoping to avoid
pain and suffering, while seeking whatever pleasures the world may
afford them. As Besant puts it, "They walk not straight onwards as
though intent on business, but wander hither and thither, like children
running after a blossom here, and chasing a butterfly there."[59] She
goes on to explain that there exist those rare souls who long ago raised
their eyes from the dusty path below to see the luminous destination
at the top of the mountain. Not content to trudge along with the

masses, they chose the more difficult path, the path of direct ascent, also known as the path of hastened unfoldment. The winding path is safer, but interminable. The vertical ascent is quicker, but perilous.

Mircea Eliade, a religious historian known for his interpretations of religious symbolism, explains that the direct ascent "is arduous, fraught with perils because it is, in fact, a rite of passage from the profane to the sacred, from the ephemeral and illusory to reality and eternity, from death to life, from man to the divinity."[60] Or, as John Milton states in *Paradise Lost,* "Long is the way and hard, that out of Hell leads up to light."[61]

Returning to Besant's image, who are those that remain in the Temple? In the Buddhist tradition, they are the Bodhisattvas who have renounced Nirvana for the express purpose of helping humanity. In the Theosophical tradition, they are the Adepts, the Mahatmas, the Masters of Wisdom, working to alleviate the suffering of humanity.

Compassion Is More Than a Virtue

Compassion is no attribute. It is the
Law of laws—eternal harmony (vs. 300).

The above excerpt is interesting for several reasons. Compassion is one of the main themes in the *Voice*, and the word itself first appears in verse 101, where it is used as an epithet: "And now, O Teacher of Compassion, point thou the way to other men." The word *compassion* appears five more times (mostly as an epithet, e.g., Buddhas of Compassion, Masters of Compassion) before resurfacing in verse 300 in somewhat climactic fashion, because it is here, near the end of the book, where it is defined for the very first time.

Another way the above excerpt stands out is that it defines compassion first in terms of what it isn't. Compare it to verses 207–211, which introduce the paramitas. You will notice that each one is defined in the usual manner, that is, by providing a description of what it is. Kshanti is "patience sweet, that nought can ruffle." Virya is "the dauntless energy that fights its way to the supernal truth out of the mire of lies terrestrial." Admittedly, these descriptions are poetic, not scholastic, but the reader still has a fair idea of what the terms represent. The declaration that compassion is not an attribute breaks this pattern by framing compassion negatively, i.e., in terms of *what it is not.* Why is this done? Is it for dramatic effect? To some extent, yes, but there is another, more important reason.

The *Shorter Oxford English Dictionary* defines *attribute* as "a quality or character ascribed to a person or thing." I have to admit that before reading the *Voice,* I would have considered compassion to be one of the attributes associated with spirituality, such as purity, generosity, or kindliness. But consider the next sentence in the opening verse: "It is the Law of laws—eternal harmony." This axiomatic statement elevates compassion beyond the category of mere attributes, however commendable they may be. It is hard to imagine anybody referring to patience or tolerance or forgiveness as laws. So why do so with compassion?

Here is my understanding. When an aspirant earnestly begins to live the spiritual life, refashioning the lower self into an instrument of the higher, a fundamental change in outlook takes place. The māyā of a separate self becomes an illusion, while the unity of all life becomes real and vivid. No longer can the sufferings of others be ignored. A sense of interconnectedness with all sentient beings gives birth to a universal sense of compassion. As a result, one can no more stem the flow of compassion than nullify the law of gravity.

A Pilgrim Has Returned!

The last few lines of *The Voice of the Silence* set a triumphant and jubilant tone:

Hark! . . . from the deep unfathomable vortex of that golden light
in which the Victor bathes, ALL NATURE'S wordless voice in
thousand tones ariseth to proclaim:

Joy unto ye, O men of Myalba.
A Pilgrim hath returned back "from the other shore."
A new Arhan is born. . . .
Peace to all beings.

This celebration is a joyous tribute to the pilgrim who, after
entering the stream many lifetimes ago, has now completed the
long and arduous journey to become a Buddha. Rather than bask
in the "Ocean of Knowledge," as Nirvana is sometimes called, this
pilgrim has chosen to remain in the world as a Buddha of Compassion, out of infinite compassion for all sentient beings.

As many have noted, the journey is indeed arduous, and the
trials are not without risks. This general depiction of those difficulties by Geoffrey Hodson comports with the warnings found
in the *Voice:*

The upward way is indeed very steep, thorny, and rocky, and it is not
unnatural that fatigue, injuries, and slips may bring about falls.[62]

A more graphic description by Hodson carries the authenticity
of one who speaks from personal experience:

During the time of preparation the candidate is made to face . . .
adverse incidents of this life and the intense humiliation and hurt
that results. It must be like a process of being "flayed alive," since
the sense of personal guilt for past errors and "falls" in the spiritually awakened Ego is, naturally, so strong. This process is invoked
by the candidate himself and consequently he must be prepared for
the painful stripping away of his past and its results, particularly
the psychological ones.[63]

Descriptions such as these are meant, not to discourage or
prevent aspirants from making the attempt, but rather to give a

sober and realistic assessment of the task that lies ahead.

Over a hundred years ago, one of Blavatsky's teachers offered a note of encouragement to a particular disciple. Short and to the point, the advice of that teacher remains timeless, and it applies to aspiring pilgrims of any time and place: "We have one word for all aspirants: TRY."[64]

Chapter 12

REFLECTIONS ON
THE SECRET DOCTRINE

Defining *Doctrine*

The word *doctrine* may be defined as set of principles or as a body of teachings related to a particular subject. One example from the field of religion would be the Calvinist doctrine of predestination. In the realm of jurisprudence, the doctrine of self-defense is well established. Economists often refer to Marxist or Keynesian doctrines. The military has its doctrines relating to warfare, which are studied at West Point and other military academies.

A doctrine is something more than an idea or even a concept. For an idea or concept to rise to the status of a doctrine, it must undergo a period of intense critical analysis by experts in that particular field. The principles articulated by Mme. Blavatsky in *The Secret Doctrine* qualify as doctrines because, as part of a centuries-old wisdom tradition, they have undergone such scrutiny.

In his historical introduction to the 1979 edition, editor Boris de Zirkoff dispenses with the notion that it is nothing more than a "syncretistic work wherein a multitude of seemingly unrelated teachings and ideas are cleverly woven together to form a more or less coherent whole" (1:74). It is not difficult to see how a novice might arrive at this superficial conclusion, given the nonlinear style of writing employed by Blavatsky in her magnum opus.

To the student possessing a measure of intuitive capacity, however, deep and sustained consideration will reveal *The Secret Doctrine* to be "a wholly coherent outline of an ageless doctrine, a system of thought based upon occult facts and universal truths inherent in nature and which are as specific and definite as any mathematical proposition" (ibid.).

Just as a Catholic theologian is conversant with the doctrine of the Holy Trinity, or an economist is knowledgeable about the doctrine of mercantilism, the serious student of the wisdom tradition strives to understand the doctrines of reincarnation, emanation, periodicity, and other esoteric principles put forth by Mme. Blavatsky in her great contribution to world thought. These are more than mere ideas or concepts; they are doctrines in the truest sense of the word.

Doctrine vs. *Dogma*

It may surprise you to learn that Theosophical literature contains some scary words, at least according to some people. One of those frightening words is *hierarchy*; another is *doctrine*. I'll deal with the former at a future date, but for now, let's consider the latter.

Why, you might ask, would the word *doctrine* make some people uneasy? It's a two-syllable word, unlike some of those hard-to-pronounce Sanskrit terms found in *The Secret Doctrine*, such as *svabhavat* or *manu-svâyambhuva*. Perhaps the words *hierarchy* and *doctrine* don't intimidate you. That's good. They don't cause me to break out in a cold sweat either, but then I'm a third-degree black belt with years of training in the martial arts.

Still, some Theosophists harbor an almost visceral dislike for certain words. I'll give you one example: Years ago, a member of the Milwaukee Lodge expressed his discomfort to me over the word *doctrine.* He mischievously threatened to get a custom-made bumper sticker reading, "My dogma ran over your doctrine." I gave him points for alliteration.

Herein lies the crux of the matter, namely, that some people equate doctrine with dogma. The truth is that doctrines do not become dogma without an element of coercion. When people are forced to accept an idea or concept without the ability to question or interpret, the result is dogma. Religions have done that. Some still do. By contrast, Theosophy has a number of metaphysical doctrines that are not, and should not, be presented in a dogmatic way. Members of the Theosophical Society are free to accept or reject them as they see fit.

The late Emily Sellon, someone I consider to have been a brilliant student of Theosophy, had this to say about Theosophical doctrines: "These are not dogmas designed to tell us how to think, but guidelines to keep us from getting lost in the wilderness of contemporary information and opinion."[1] Rightly understood, a well-articulated doctrine serves as a beacon of light that guides our quest for deeper understanding. Dogma, however, shackles the mind and results in a state of intellectual darkness and paralysis. Now, to me, *that's* scary!

Defining *Secret*

A secret may be defined as something known only to a few. But who doesn't enjoy being privy to one, only to turn around and share that "secret" with another? There's a clever line from a seventeenth-century play: "I know that's a secret for it's whispered everywhere."[2] Another definition of the word *secret* is "an unexplained or inscrutable process or fact." Still another refers to the knowledge of an esoteric society, which is concealed or veiled from the gaze of the uninitiated.

The reader of *The Secret Doctrine* learns that "this book is not the Secret Doctrine in its entirety, but a select number of fragments of its fundamental tenets" (1:viii).[3] This is due to the fact that "not even the greatest living adept" was allowed to "give out promiscuously, to a mocking, unbelieving world, that which has been so effectually concealed from it for long aeons and ages." (1:xviii). But in the late nineteenth century, a few custodians of the wisdom tradition felt the time was ripe to lift "a small corner of the dark veil" (1:xvii) for the benefit of humankind. With permission from their superiors, they collaborated with Helena Petrovna Blavatsky to do exactly that.

Blavatsky states in the preface that "what is contained in this work is to be found scattered throughout thousands of volumes embodying the scriptures of the great Asiatic and early European religions, hidden under glyph and symbol, and hitherto left unnoticed because of this veil" (1:vii). So, in one sense, this information was already available to those who had the will to seek and the eyes to see—and the time to do the research.

The Secret Doctrine also hints at sublime realities beyond the limited scope of words or rational thought. "Only those who realize how far Intuition soars above the tardy processes of ratiocinative thought," says HPB, "can form the faintest conception of the absolute Wisdom which transcends the ideas of Time and Space" (1:1 fn).

And this is why Blavatsky's magnum opus continues to intrigue, enchant, and inspire, more than a hundred years after its initial publication. No matter how often one studies or discusses this monumental exposition of occult doctrines, an elusive but beckoning element remains, the essence of which is not only beyond speech but beyond even the merest shadow of a whisper. The real secrets alluded to in *The Secret Doctrine* cannot be shared or disseminated, but they may be discovered.

Collaborative Effort

Through her vast store of occult knowledge, her unwavering dedication, and her unique mental and psychic abilities, Blavatsky served as a messenger for the Great Ones in the service of humanity. Perhaps her preeminent accomplishment was the publication of *The Secret Doctrine*, a work of monumental scope and dimension. But in this undertaking, she did not work alone. The evidence suggests a collaborative effort in which HPB served as the conscious vehicle for various Adepts and advanced students of the wisdom tradition.

The question that is sometimes asked is, why the secrecy? Why don't the Adepts come forth publicly and make their existence known? In fact, there are good reasons for their self-imposed seclusion from the prying eyes of the world, but within this limited space, allow me to provide just one such explanation.

If any true Adept were to come forth publicly in today's materialistic world, the results would be most unfortunate. An unprepared and skeptical public might react to such an event in one of two ways: one faction would engage in blind worship, while another would react with overt hostility and vicious condemnation.

In 1880, A. P. Sinnett, a colleague of Blavatsky's, tried to persuade one of the Adepts to abandon the age-old policy of secrecy. Sinnett received this reply:

> In common with many, you blame us for our great secrecy. Yet we know something of human nature, for the experience of long centuries—aye, ages—has taught us. And we know, that so long as science has anything to learn, and a shadow of religious dogmatism lingers in the hearts of the multitudes, the world's prejudices have to be conquered step by step, not at a rush. As hoary antiquity had more than one Socrates, so the dim Future will give birth to more than one martyr.[4]

And so, the Great Ones will continue to work under the radar, so to speak, for the benefit of a world that is not quite ready to acknowledge its unseen benefactors.

We Are Greater Than We Know

"How little do we know that which we are! How less what we may be!"[5] These lines from Byron's *Don Juan* are as true today as when they were first published in the 1820s. Our sense of identity is formed by many factors—our parents, the prevailing culture, the media, etc. No sensible person would deny the role these and other influences play in shaping our personalities. Yet to circumscribe our sense of self to the limited scope of empirical factors is to ignore our true essence. It's like my saying I understand the ocean because I've skimmed its surface in a small boat.

There is a profound mystery at the core of our being, one that cannot be discounted by all the statistics favored by scientists, psychologists, and sociologists. Their work has value, but it doesn't explain the mystery of our being. As William Wordsworth observed, "We feel that we are greater than we know."[6]

Consider the often-quoted phrase from the third Fundamental Proposition of *The Secret Doctrine*, asserting "the fundamental identity of all Souls with the Universal Over-Soul" (1:17). The term *Over-Soul* appears in an essay published in 1841 by Emerson, in which he says: "It is undefinable, unmeasurable; but we know that it pervades and contains us."[7] If it cannot be measured or defined, then whatever this Over-Soul is would be, by definition, beyond the reach of scientific knowledge. Yet Emerson claims we *know* of its presence. Fine, but *how* do we know? May I suggest that we know of the Over-Soul, not in the ordinary sense, such as knowing that two plus two equals four, but rather by an intuitive perception.

Notice the choice of words used in the third proposition. The relation of the soul to the Over-Soul is characterized not as a mere likeness, resemblance, or similarity but in terms of *fundamental identity*. That's significant. Consider, for a moment, the difference between sharing a similarity versus sharing a fundamental identity with something. An apple may resemble an orange in that they are both round and grow on trees, but nobody confuses the two. They share similarities, but they are not identical.

To understand the nature of the ocean requires more than skimming its surface. Dwelling on our personality quirks and preferences is like skimming the surface of a vast body of water. Discovering the mystery at the heart of our being, say the sages, requires diving into the depths of human consciousness. Then one may come to know what one truly is.

Theosophy: A Living Tradition

H. P. Blavatsky firmly maintained that the doctrines presented in *The Secret Doctrine* were not new fabrications flowing from her prolific pen but an integral part of an esoteric tradition with a pedigree extending back thousands of years. To support this controversial claim, she sprinkled her masterwork with a bevy of historical figures from antiquity who were associated with Theosophical ideas. One example is Anaxagoras of Clazomenae, an obscure name from ancient Greek history. He was the tutor of Pericles, the famed and respected Athenian statesman and general who lived during the time of Socrates. Blavatsky mentions Anaxagoras several times in *The Secret Doctrine* and once in *The Key to Theosophy*. The Roman historian Plutarch says that Anaxagoras

> was the first of the philosophers who did not refer the first ordering of the world to fortune or chance, nor to necessity or compulsion,

but to a pure, unadulterated intelligence, which in all other existing mixed and compound things acts as a principle of discrimination, and of combination of like with like.[8]

Plutarch says that Pericles held his tutor in the highest regard
and that the influence of Anaxagoras and his teachings upon
Pericles resulted not only in an "elevation of purpose and dignity
of language, raised far above the base and dishonest buffooner-
ies of mob-eloquence." Anaxagoras also displayed "a composure of
countenance and a serenity and a calmness in all his movements,
which no occurrence whilst he was speaking could disturb; a sustained and even tone of voice, and various other advantages of a
similar kind, which produced the greatest effect on his hearers."[9]

Theosophical doctrines may be part of a tradition dating back
centuries, but they also speak to our times, just as they will continue to speak to future generations. Whereas some ideas from
the past are nothing more than dust in the corridors of time, the
timeless principles espoused in *The Secret Doctrine* have the power
to radically transform the manner in which we react and interact
with the world about us.

Mundane Secrets and Transcendent Mysteries

When peering down at city streets from atop a metropolitan sky-
scraper, one has the curious sense of viewing humanity from a
broader perspective as well as from an elevated position. Far below,
between the towering canyons of concrete and steel, a river of humanity is in motion, an incessant movement of people going about
their business, carrying with them their immediate concerns, their
hopes and fears, their private thoughts and innermost secrets.

What kind of secrets? All kinds: a loving husband plans on surprising his wife with a bouquet of flowers; a calculating business-

man broods over his unveiled marketing strategy; a shy teenage girl vows she will never tell her friends about her awful blind date the night before; a frustrated school teacher has quietly decided to revise her resume without telling her coworkers. Secrets come in all forms; some are short lived, while others are taken to the grave; some are benign, while others are dark and malevolent.

Beyond the secrets harbored on the surface of our consciousness, there is something that exists at a much deeper level, something that is properly termed a *mystery*. Emerson alluded to it when he said, "Man is a stream whose source is hidden."[10] Secrets are known, at least to the possessor; they can be revealed or explained. A true mystery, however, can never be fully explained to the satisfaction of the rational mind. In *The Secret Doctrine*, Blavatsky establishes the bedrock principle of "the fundamental identity of all Souls with the Universal Over-Soul" (1:17). This is a profound and impenetrable mystery, one that lies beyond the scope of the biologist, neurologist, or geneticist. It cannot be explained by genetic codes, neurological maps, or physiological relationships. It is a true mystery.

Secrets come and go. Like a river transporting debris downstream, we carry our secrets with us until such time as they are divulged or discovered or purged from our consciousness. By contrast, the timeless mystery of human existence remains, not as some transient event hovering on the periphery of our consciousness but at the very core of our being.

Bridging the Gap

From where does inspiration arise? I'm talking not about ordinary emotional impulses but about that rare energy that originates from otherworldly realms, bringing with it the power to elevate consciousness and propel one to engage in altruistic action.

Great composers have the ability to hear celestial sounds and transmute them into music that can be heard by ordinary people. In a letter written in 1823 to a younger musician, Beethoven touched upon the mystery of inspiration: "You will ask where my ideas come from. I cannot say for certain. They come uncalled, sometimes independently, sometimes in association with other things."[11]

Some of Beethoven's greatest accomplishments, particularly his symphonies, the late string quartets, and certain piano sonatas, were inspired by archetypal ideas. Somehow, Beethoven was able to bring these sublime forces into expression on the physical plane, thereby elevating and enrichening the consciousness of millions. Was he not a prime example of what in *The Voice of the Silence* H. P. Blavatsky called becoming a coworker with nature (vs. 66)?

There is a fundamental duality pervading the manifested universe. *The Secret Doctrine* uses archetypal terms such as *subject* and *object*, *spirit* and *matter*, *life* and *form* when referring to this dualistic principle. The task of the inspired artist is to bridge the gap between these two worlds, the world of sublime ideas and the world of concrete expression. The creative process is said to be 10 percent inspiration and 90 percent perspiration. If, for example, a composer has not spent time and effort learning the capabilities and limitations of musical instruments, if he is not well versed in harmonic theory and methods of melodic development, then whatever inspiration comes his way will be largely wasted, because his efforts to reflect the original inspiration in terms of music will be awkward and ineffectual.

Do we see the analogy to the spiritual life? Is not this proportionality of effort to inspiration also true for it? *The Secret Doctrine* states that not one individual soul can "escape its unconscious mission, or get rid of the burden of its cooperative work with nature" (2:446). If we provide the 90 percent, the 10 percent will come to us of its own accord.

No Apology Needed

It's a familiar refrain: "I've tried reading *The Secret Doctrine*, but it was too difficult." Longtime members of the Society are familiar with this complaint; some have even felt the need to apologize for the difficulty of HPB's magnum opus.

No one familiar with *The Secret Doctrine* would characterize it as an easy read. The truth is that it *is* difficult. In an age when instant results and easy accessibility are considered virtues, this monumental work stands as a sober reminder that coming to terms with greatness is neither quick nor easy.

There is a parallel, I think, to great music. In a March 21, 2012 interview with *The Wall St. Journal*, the chairman of the organ department at the Julliard School of Music, Paul Jacobs, said, "There's no denying that the music of the great masters of the past makes demands upon listeners. However, today classical musicians constantly apologize for these demands in an effort to be listener-friendly. But great music needs no apology."

Amen to that. Many Theosophical books have been published over the years, some of average quality, others of a noticeably higher caliber, and a select few that may be classified as great literature, i.e., works that have staying power from one genera-tion to the next, distinguished by their literary style as well as by their substance. In my humble opinion, and in the view of many Theosophical scholars, *The Secret Doctrine* meets those standards of greatness.

So let us freely acknowledge that HPB's magnum opus presents a challenge for most readers. It is probably unlike any other book you or I will read in our lifetime. But at the same time, let us not make excuses for its difficulty, just as no musician should feel ob-ligated to make amends for the music of Beethoven or Bach. With regard to *The Secret Doctrine*, we will not be able to hear its hidden melodies or attune to its cosmic harmonies without putting forth mental effort. And for those who are unwilling to do that, its music will forever fall upon deaf ears.

Why the Secrecy?

For long ages, the esoteric teachings of the wisdom tradition were transmitted in guarded secrecy by Initiates to their pupils. In the late nineteenth century, a few Guardians of the Wisdom felt the time was ripe to reach a broader audience. As their chosen agent, H. P. Blavatsky was allowed to "raise but a small corner of the dark veil" (1:xvii) through the publication of *The Secret Doctrine*. Prior to that time, no Initiate was allowed to "give out promiscuously, to a mocking, unbelieving world" (ibid.) the sacred teachings that had been concealed from the masses for so long.

We live in a democratic age where secrecy and confidentiality are often suspect, while transparency and openness are considered virtues. It's also a time when having near-instant access to all sorts of data is taken for granted. Therefore, one who is unfamiliar with the wisdom tradition and the mystery schools of antiquity may be excused for asking, "Why the secrecy? Why lift only a portion of the veil instead of giving out all of it? Why not release all esoteric knowledge for the benefit of the world?"

At the risk of sounding judgmental, the short answer is that the world is not yet ready. Ours is a world still steeped in ignorance, superstition, and selfishness, despite the brilliance of our technological advances. In a letter written in 1880, one of the aforementioned Guardians explained to his impatient pupil: "The world's prejudices have to be conquered step by step, not at a rush."[12] It's relatively easy for people to adapt to new technologies but infinitely difficult to change established ways of thinking. The seventeenth-century philosopher John Locke noted that "new opinions are always suspected, and usually opposed, without any other reason but because they are not already common."13 In a statement widely attributed to Voltaire, the French writer quipped, "Prejudices are what fools use for reason." The British politician Edmund Burke wrote, "Superstition is the religion of feeble minds."14

With her publication of *The Secret Doctrine,* H. P. Blavatsky lifted a small portion of the veil for the benefit of humankind. What the world does with those teachings will determine whether and when a subsequent unveiling will occur.

St. Augustine's Dilemma

The opening stanza of *The Secret Doctrine* stops the rational mind dead in its tracks: "Time was not, for it lay asleep in the Infinite Bosom of Duration." The rational mind wants to ask, "How can there not be time?" But what is time? We generally understand it as *past, present,* and *future*—this threefold division corresponding to the way we experience the world. Upon closer examination, however, the concept of time proves to be one of the most illusory aspects of phenomenal existence.

Mme. Blavatsky was not the first to point this out. Consider this passage of Augustine's in his *Confessions*:

> For what is time? Who can even comprehend it in thought or put the answer into words? . . . How is it that there are the two times, past and future, when even the past is now no longer and the future is now not yet? But if the present were always present, and did not pass into past time, it obviously would not be time but eternity.15

The Secret Doctrine describes the present as "a mathematical line which divides that part of eternal duration which we call the future, from that part which we call the past" (1:37). A true mathematical line has no existence in this three-dimensional world.

What you see on the draftsman's schematic is only a reasonable representation of it, for a mathematical line exists only in the realm of ideas, not in the world of form. Let us return to the *Confessions* of Augustine:

> If any fraction of time be conceived that cannot now be divided even into the most minute momentary point, this alone is what we may call time present. But this flies so rapidly from future to past that it cannot be extended by any delay. For if it is extended, it is then divided into past and future. But the present has no extension whatsoever.[16]

The rational mind reels in bewilderment before all this. Perhaps it was Marcus Aurelius who put it best: "Every instant of time [is] a pinprick of eternity."[17]

An Antidote for Modern Ailments

Spending a few hours with *The Secret Doctrine* can be an effective antidote for the maladies of modern life, some of which include a myopic perspective wherein small events loom large; a feeling that one's existence serves no greater purpose than utilitarian ends; a compulsion to pursue immediate pleasures at the expense of lasting values; and an increasingly combative approach in a world marked by factions, partisanship, and adversarial relationships.

In a world of almost seven billion people, of what significance is one person? And without a deep sense of purpose, can one be fully human? In Marguerite Yourcenar's historical novel, *Memoirs of Hadrian*, the Roman emperor Hadrian arrived at this insight:

> The mind of man is reluctant to consider itself as the product of chance, or the passing result of destinies over which no god presides, least of all himself. A part of every life, even a life meriting

little regard, is spent in searching out the reasons for its existence, its starting point, and its source.[18]

Modern life, with its intrusive media and rapid technological change, creates the sense of time being compressed, of events speeding up, gaining momentum and even careening out of control, all of which compels us to feel that we are being swept along relentlessly by blind and impersonal forces to destinations unknown.

By contrast, *The Secret Doctrine* provides us with a broad and timeless perspective by speaking of eternity and the illusory nature of time; by describing grand evolutionary cycles of immense magnitude; by restoring knowledge of our fundamental identity with the divine Principle. An understanding of these principles serves as an effective palliative to the ills of modern life. As these teachings are assimilated, the sense of hopelessness dissipates. Outer circumstances lose their power to disturb us, and no longer do we feel divided and isolated from the rest of humanity.

> Nothing in the world is single;
> All things by a law divine
> In one spirit meet and mingle.
> —Percy Blythe Shelley,
> "Love's Philosophy"

A Fool's Errand

Unless one is an illumined sage, the writer who proposes to expatiate upon the Absolute runs the risk of being seen as either a pious pontificator or an innocent naïf. To speak at length about that which is "unspeakable" is likely a fool's errand. Prudence would suggest the safest course of action to be one that defers to the

wisdom of those seers who have had a rare glimpse into the nature
of the ultimate Reality:

> The ever unchangeable is devoid of sound, touch, form, taste or
> smell. It is without beginning or end, ever beyond the prime cause
> of all evolution.
>
> —Katha Upanishad[19]

> There the eye goes not, speech goes not, nor the mind.
>
> —Kena Upanishad[20]

> The Absolute is described as "not this," "not that," and so on
> by negatives only.
>
> —Brihadaranyaka Upanishad[21]

As HPB states in *The Secret Doctrine*, the Absolute is an "Immutable PRINCIPLE on which all speculation is impossible" (1:14).
It is, she says, "not to be defined, and no mortal or immortal has
ever seen or comprehended it," and further, "the mutable cannot
know the Immutable" (2:34). For against the impenetrable shroud
of mystery surrounding the Absolute, all attempts at rigorous intellectual inquiry inevitably yield to a state of flaccid impotence.

But before we dismiss further reflection on the Absolute as ut-
terly useless, we might consider what G. de Purucker, a serious
student of *The Secret Doctrine*, said in this regard: "We are taught
that there exists in man a link with the Unutterable, a cord, a communication, that extends from It to the inner consciousness."[22]
And this from I. K. Taimni: "The fact that it is called 'Unknowable' does not mean that it is beyond the range of philosophical or
religious thought and something on which thinking is impossible
or undesirable. . . . It is unknowable and yet the highest object
of realization, unthinkable and yet the most profound object of
philosophical enquiry."[23]

And so, with this brief missive, this humble scribe hopes that he has successfully walked the fine line between naiveté and flap-doodle. For at his age, the former would be unseemly, and the latter would embarrass his dear mother, who was not in the habit of raising fools.

A Flight of Fancy

Space is the one eternal thing that we can most easily imagine,
immovable in its abstraction and uninfluenced by either the
presence or absence in it of an objective Universe (1:135).

Imagine this: You're suspended in interstellar space . . . alone . . . when suddenly the stars begin to disappear. Within seconds, not only stars but entire constellations and galaxies are gone—vanished without a trace. All that remains is an unfathomable darkness, an uncompromising stillness, terrifying in its absoluteness. There's no gravity, no *up* or *down*, no *in* or *out*, no *here* or *there*. Those words are now devoid of meaning, relics of a nonexistent world. Your mind races for a rational explanation, peering into the opaque abyss, anxiously searching for some discrete object . . . something . . . anything . . . anywhere.

It's a total blackout, a mute blackness unlike anything you've ever imagined. You feel the unnerving sensation of a boy on his first roller-coaster ride. Are you moving? Are you suspended? You could be tumbling headlong into the bowels of infinity, but how would you know? Without any visible points of reference, is there such a thing as motion? A subtle and diabolical thought arises: *Maybe the cloak of darkness extends only a few yards in all directions.* Claustrophobia and panic! You want to escape. This screen of oppressive opacity is causing you to lose your grip. What is reality? What happened to the world as you knew it? All that your conditioned mind was accustomed to has passed into oblivion.

In a while, you recall something you once read in *The Secret Doctrine* about cosmic cycles and the dissolution of the cosmos. That's it—a cosmic Pralaya in which time no longer exists and darkness fills the boundless ALL! What you are experiencing is the sense of being in space prior to the manifestation of the universe.

With this realization, you begin to acclimate yourself to the void. In this mysterious nothingness, without objects or events to stimulate thought, the mind grows still. There's only absolute silence . . . and utter darkness. Releasing all thoughts, memories, and dreams, you sink into the soft bosom of infinite duration, blissfully surrendering yourself to a dreamless sleep, a sleep that will last for seven eternities.

Defining *Emanation*

One of the oldest questions asked by inquiring minds may be this: "How did the world come into being?" Christian theologians subscribe to the doctrine of *creatio ex nihilo*, the belief that God created the universe out of nothing. An opposing doctrine, *ex nihilo nihil fit*—from nothing, nothing is produced—was expressed by the Roman philosopher Lucretius in his epic poem *On the Nature of Things*:

> But only Nature's aspect and her law,
> Which, teaching us, hath this exordium:
> Nothing from nothing ever yet was born.

There is also *creatio ex deo*, the idea that the cosmos was created out of the being of God:

> Before the world existed, the Self Alone existed; nothing whatever stirred. Then the Self thought: "Let me create the world." He brought forth all the worlds out of himself
>
> —Aitareya Upanishad[24]

And then there is *creatio ex materia*, the idea that the cosmos was created out of some eternal and preexistent type of matter by a divine being or principle. Proponents of these doctrines agree on one thing—the universe exists. How it came into existence is where they part company. So, what does Theosophy say?

In a word, *emanation*. The term is from the Latin, meaning "to flow out from." It implies an unfolding from within to without; from potential to actual; from the latent to the manifest. "No one creates the universe. Scientists call the process evolution. Theosophists call it emanation."[25] "The doctrine of Emanation was at one time universal. It was taught by the Alexandrian as well as by the Indian philosophers, by the Egyptian, the Chaldean and Hellenic Hierophants, and also by the Hebrews."[26] But as Blavatsky observed in *The Secret Doctrine*, Christian theology long ago "rejected the doctrine of emanations and replaced them with direct, conscious creations of angels and the rest out of *nothing*" (2:41).

In the Upanishads, the appearance and disappearance of the universe has been depicted as the Great Breath, its emergence symbolized by the outward breath, its dissolution by the inward breath. In Sanskrit, the word signifying the manifestation of a universe following its dissolution is *manvantara*. The process is without beginning or end; it is a cycle that repeats endlessly.

And so it is that in a remote galaxy of a future manvantara far, far away, inquisitive minds will again ask the perennial question: "How did the universe come into being?"

Defining *Logos*

Central to the metaphysics of *The Secret Doctrine* is the Logos doctrine. The word *logos* comes to us from the Greek, meaning "reason" or "word." As an aside, one might speculate on why Blavatsky chose such a uniquely Western term, as opposed to other options found in Eastern philosophy, in order to convey such a fundamental concept. Be that as it may, an excellent definition of *logos* is found in *Webster's Third New International Dictionary*:

> **Logos:** reason or the manifestation of reason conceived in ancient Greek philosophy as constituting the controlling principle in the universe; a moving and regulating principle in the universe together with an element in man by which according to Heraclitus this principle is perceived; a cosmic governing or generating principle according to the Stoics that is immanent and active in all reality and pervades all reality.

As an active principle, the Logos is impersonal and universal. The Greeks understood it to be a creative energy, not an entity or being. It later became personalized in Christian theology as the second Person (*verbum*) of the Trinity. A post-Blavatsky generation of Theosophists, including Besant and Leadbeater, also personalized the Logos in their writings. But you will not find this in *The Secret Doctrine*, where it is presented symbolically as the point within the circle, the circle representing the boundless ALL, the point representing "the first differentiation in the periodical manifestations" (1:4) known poetically as the Days and Nights of Brahman. It's an apt symbol, since a point is without size or dimension. *The Secret Doctrine* elaborates:

> This Point is the First Cause, but THAT from which it emanates, or of which, rather, it is the expression, the Logos, is passed over in silence. In its turn, the universal symbol, the *point within the circle*, was not yet the Architect, but the cause of that Architect; and the latter stood to it in precisely the same relation as the point itself stood to the *circumference* of the Circle, which cannot be defined, according to Hermes Trismegistus (2:426).

Students of *The Secret Doctrine* are well advised to make the attempt at understanding the Logos doctrine, so vital and so central is it to the metaphysics of Theosophy.

Three Aspects of Logos

The appearance and disappearance of the universe is cyclical and ongoing. In *The Key to Theosophy*, H. P. Blavatsky states: "It is an eternal and periodical law which causes an active and creative force (the logos) to emanate from the ever-concealed and incomprehensible one principle at the beginning of every . . . new cycle of life."[27] Notice that Blavatsky characterizes the impetus behind the emanation of a new universe as a "creative force," thereby implying the presence of intelligence. Whatever the nature of that mysterious force may be, it is certainly not "blind" or mechanical.

This creative force is universally acknowledged to have three aspects, which in religious circles are thought of as a trinity. For example, we have the Father, Son, and Holy Ghost of Christianity; Osiris, Isis, and Horus in the religion of ancient Egypt; and Brahma, Vishnu, and Siva in Hinduism. Theosophy does not use any of these terms but instead uses the Greek term *logos*. This threefold force is referred to in *The Secret Doctrine* as the First, Second, and Third Logos. It should be noted that these are to be thought of not as three separate Logoi but as three aspects of one divine Principle.

> The [First Logos] is the already present yet still unmanifested potentiality . . . the Second is the abstract collectivity of creators called "Demiurgi" by the Greeks or the Builders of the Universe. The *third logos* is the ultimate differentiation of the Second and the individualization of Cosmic Forces.[28]

So, what we have is the Unmanifest, the manifested, and the "bridge" between the two states. Further insight is provided by one of the great students of *The Secret Doctrine*, Geoffrey Barborka:

The First Logos is equivalent to the First Point of the system, or the causative aspect; it represents the fount and origin of the forces and potencies that will be surging forth into manifestation. However, this First Point itself will ever remain unmanifest. Hence it is termed the Unmanifest Logos. In order that the forces and potencies may be made manifest upon a material plane they must be transmitted from the unmanifest aspect to a manifested aspect. This transmittal is accomplished by means of the Second Logos, which . . . provides the link, or bridge, between the non-manifest and the manifested plane. The point of origin on the manifested plane is regarded as the Third Logos . . . which is also regarded as the Creative Logos.[29]

Barborka's comparison of the Unmanifest Logos to a point is interesting. A true mathematical point has absolutely no width, length, or height; in other words, it has no dimensionality and therefore cannot exist in our three-dimensional world. How can you or I comprehend something that cannot exist in our world of space and form? To this end, Barborka also offers a helpful simile:

The First Logos represents the idea; the Second Logos, the formulation and the means of expressing the idea through speech and words; the Third Logos, the expression of the idea by means of spoken words. And yet, even when the words have been spoken the First Logos, or idea, is still "unmanifest."[30]

And thus, the invisible becomes visible and latent potentialities become actualized, all of which may be represented symbolically as the primordial point becoming the archetypal triangle.

As Above, So Below

Some students of *The Secret Doctrine* may wonder what relevance the Logos doctrine has to daily life. They find it to be a fascinating concept but one that seems far off, remote, with little bearing on the here and now. As a metaphysical explanation for how the universe came into being, they see its value; yet at the same time they wonder if such knowledge is of any real practical use. To answer this query, we should stipulate that the Logos is a universal principle, immanent in the manifested universe, and therefore a part of all life. To study the Logos doctrine is to learn about ourselves. The microcosm reflects the macrocosm: as above, so below. In his *Occult Glossary*, G. de Purucker explains:

> *Logos* is a word having several applications in the Esoteric Philosophy, for there are different kinds or grades of logoi, some of them of divine, some of them of a spiritual character; some of them having a cosmic range, and others . . . much more restricted. In fact, every individual entity, no matter what its evolutionary grade on the ladder of life, has its own individual Logos. . . . Small or great as every solar system may be, each has its own Logos, the source or fountainhead of almost innumerable logoi of less degree in that system.[31]

We may recall that the First, Second, and Third Logoi are not three separate beings but names used to represent three aspects of a Unity. This is reflected in the human being as *Atma-Buddhi-Manas*, variously referred to in *The Secret Doctrine* as the Heavenly Man, the spiritual Triad, or the immortal Ego. Atma in the human expresses itself as spiritual will, corresponding to the First Logos; Buddhi as compassionate wisdom or love, as with the Second Logos; Manas as reason and creative activity, as with the Third Logos. When we create, when we love, when we exercise our spiritual will, we are exercising innate and divine powers, all of which will grow in strength and splendor as we continue our long pilgrimage throughout a series of deaths and rebirths on the great stage of life.

The Cosmic Ladder of Life

One of the more fascinating themes in *The Secret Doctrine* is that of hierarchy. The English language confines the word *hierarchy* mainly to ecclesiastical matters, and so the general public remains unaware of its occult denotations. Due to its association in the public mind with priestly matters, the term carries certain negative connotations—rigidity, dominance, and exploitation, for instance. But the esoteric meaning of *hierarchy* as presented in *The Secret Doctrine* is one that inspires awe and wonder, revealing a hidden natural order involving various planes, or levels, of existence as well as a vast multitude of beings. This panoramic view has been described by at least one writer as the cosmic ladder of life.[32]

The strange-sounding names of the hierarchical beings appearing on the pages of Mme. Blavatsky's magnum opus read like the cast of a Federico Fellini film: Architects, Builders, and Silent Watchers; Kumaras and Pitris and Agnishvattas; Elementals, Asuras, and Dhyân-Chohans; Lipikas and Lahs and Mânasaputras. All this is likely to leave the first-time reader feeling as bewildered as a Norwegian cook who stumbles into an Indian spice shop. But with continued study the names grow familiar, and their respective roles come into focus. It gradually becomes clear that each planetary or celestial being has its special role to play in the greater economy of the divine plan.

Some may find the idea of a cosmic hierarchy to be fanciful, if not preposterous. But is it really? Consider, for example, a large corporation employing tens of thousands of people. It is structured so that its manifold operations—finance and accounting, advertising and marketing, engineering and production, research and development—are all set up as separate departments run by competent managers, whose business it is to see that each unit carries out its part smoothly and efficiently. We live in an intelligent and purposeful universe. "As above, so below," says the Hermetic axiom. If a mere human enterprise recognizes the value of organization, should we expect any less of the universe?

Celestial Scribes

The cast of actors entering and exiting the pages of *The Secret Doctrine* includes some of the most elusive and mysterious characters you could imagine. Take, for instance, the Lipikas. Who are they? And what do they do? The reader is provided with precious little information—just enough to arouse curiosity. Scholars explain that the word *Lipika* comes from the Sanskrit verbal root *lip*, meaning to write, to inscribe, to engrave, which is why the Lipikas are sometimes called Recorders, Scribes, or Annalists—names meant to be taken not literally but metaphorically. Theosophists commonly refer to them as the Lords of Karma.

According to the author of *The Secret Doctrine*, "These Divine Beings are connected with Karma . . . [They keep] a faithful record of every act, and even thought, of man, of all that was, is, or ever will be, in the phenomenal Universe. As said in *Isis*, this divine and unseen canvas is the BOOK OF LIFE" (1:104).

Commentators provide additional insights. According to Annie Besant, "They hold the threads of destiny which each man has woven, and guide the reincarnating man to the environment determined by his past."33 G. de Purucker says, "They are infinitely more impersonal and more automatic in their action than are the recorders in a court of law, setting down word by word, act by act, whatever takes place in the cosmic courtroom; and their record is infinitely accurate and just. There is no personal equation at all."34 And Geoffrey Barborka has this to say: "Each one may add to his own 'Book of Life.' In fact, everyone is doing so, whether a person is aware of it or not."35

One more thing bears mention. No human word or deed goes unnoticed by these Cosmic Scribes. In human affairs, people sometimes manage to evade accountability for their actions in the court of public opinion or in the realm of jurisprudence, but not so with Karma. For the Lipikas never take a vacation; they are on

the job, so to speak, day and night. At the dawn of a new manvantara, they are the first to appear; and as Universal Day yields to
Universal Night, they are the last ones there to turn off the lights.

Delightful Detours

Like billboards flanking the sides of the freeway, certain major
themes such as polarity and cyclicity appear repeatedly along the
avenues of thought permeating *The Secret Doctrine*. As with the
casual traveler who exits the interstate highway in favor of rustic
back roads, it is often in a passing reference, or stray footnote, that
a slight detour into unfamiliar territory rewards the inquisitive
reader with the joy of discovery.

One detour worth taking is the consideration of the term *laya*,
which variously appears as laya-center, laya-state, or zero-point.
Laya is a Sanskrit word meaning "vanishing point" and is derived
from the verb-root *Lî*, meaning "to dissolve" or "to disintegrate."
The laya-centers described in *The Secret Doctrine* involve the sudden disappearance of planets and universes. No, they are not to
be compared with the black holes of our modern cosmologists,
nor are they the products of a creative literary mind, analogous to
the famed rabbit hole of *Alice in Wonderland*. They are something
altogether different.

Blavatsky describes the laya-state as "that point where substance
becomes homogeneous and is unable to act or differentiate."[36] The
"ever-invisible robes" spoken of in the opening sloka of the Stanzas
of Dzyan refers to primordial matter in its undifferentiated state
during the state of universal Pralaya (from the Sanskrit prefix *pra*,
meaning "away," and *laya*, meaning "to dissolve" or "dissolve away").
Stanza VI cites the creation of seven laya-centers as part of the for-
mation of the new universe. Sanskrit scholar Judith Tyberg describes
them as "channels through which consciousness or life-atoms

pass when going from one plane to another . . . they are like doors which lead in two directions."[37] Or, as Purucker puts it, they are "canals of both egress and ingress" for every kind of entity that exists, whether a man, a planet, or a sun.[38] "When a planet dies," says Blavatsky, "its informing principles are transferred to a *laya* or sleeping centre" (1:147). So, as you make your journey through *The Secret Doctrine*, don't hesitate to take an occasional detour onto the back roads, where the mystery of the unknown awaits.

Defining *Māyā*

The sight of the sun rising in the east and setting in the west, the sound of a train whistle dropping in pitch as the locomotive rushes past, the sense of a chair or table or plate as being solid— all these are easily recognized as sensory illusions. We know the appearance of the sun traversing the sky to be an optical illusion, the precipitous drop in pitch of a passing locomotive whistle to be an auditory illusion, and the seeming solidity of physical objects to be an aggregate of atoms and molecules consisting mostly of empty space.

Other illusions are not so easily discerned, especially those of a psychological nature, e.g., the belief that our perceptions of other people constitute reality, the notion that fame and celebrity have intrinsic value, the assumption that wealth leads to happiness, or the tendency to elevate our personal opinions to the level of indisputable fact. The human condition is subject to illusions of various kinds, many of which we are blissfully unaware of.

"From the standpoint of the highest metaphysics," according to Blavatsky in *The Secret Doctrine*, "the whole Universe, gods included, is an illusion" (1:329). This is the much misunderstood doctrine of Māyā, an integral part of the Esoteric Philosophy. The word *māyā* comes from the Sanskrit root *mā*, which means "to measure" or "to mark off." To say that the universe is a māyā is not to say that it doesn't exist. In this case, "temporary appearance" might be a better rendition than "illusion." Judith Tyberg defines māyā as "that which limits or circumscribes, and prevents us from cognizing perfect Truth or Reality, which is beyond limits, boundless. Māyā is the inevitable result of manifestation because matter of any kind is a veil which hides Reality. The thicker the veil, the greater the Māyā."[39]

And Blavatsky has this to say: "The Universe is called, with everything in it, MĀYĀ, because all is temporary therein, from the ephemeral life of a firefly to that of the Sun . . . Yet, the Universe is real enough to the conscious beings in it, which are as unreal as it is itself" (1:274).

This is what may be called the cosmological interpretation of Māyā, a doctrine of great profundity and multiple levels of meaning, which will become clearer to the earnest student as he or she patiently reflects on such statements, allowing the intellect to be guided by the sure light of the intuitive faculty.

A Mystery of Our Own Making

This series of essays on *The Secret Doctrine* would be incomplete if it did not include a consideration of Karma. One reason is that its descriptions of Karma contain some of its most moving and majestic language. Secondly, Karma, together with reincarnation, helps to explain many of life's apparent injustices. Here are two powerful passages from Blavatsky's prolific pen:

> We stand bewildered before the mystery of our own making, and the riddles of life that *we will not* solve, and then accuse the great Sphinx of devouring us. But verily there is not an accident in our lives, not a misshapen day, or a misfortune, that could not be traced back to our own doings in this or in another life. . . . It is

not, therefore, Karma that rewards or punishes, but it is we, who reward or punish ourselves according to whether we work with, through and along with nature, abiding by the laws on which that Harmony depends, or—break them (1:643–44).

Contrary to Old Testament descriptions of an angry and jealous deity that punishes evildoers and rewards the faithful, Blavatsky depicts Karma as an impersonal and universal law, which is to say that it operates like any other law—without showing malice or favoritism. To clothe this truth in biblical garb, it might be said that Karma "is no respecter of persons."[40] Today we live in a world where great economic, cultural, and political forces are at play, sometimes giving the impression that the individual is helpless in the face of such sweeping and relentless change. However, Blavatsky emphasizes that a human being is not a helpless victim or impotent pawn in the game of life.

> Those who believe in *Karma* have to believe in *destiny*, which, from birth to death, every man is weaving thread by thread around himself, as a spider does his cobweb. . . . When the last strand is woven, and man is seemingly enwrapped in the network of his own doing, then he finds himself completely under the empire of this *self-made* destiny. It then either fixes him like the inert shell against the immovable rock, or carries him away like a feather in a whirlwind raised by his own actions, and this is—KARMA (1:639).

This "self-made destiny" is not to be confused with fatalism, a philosophy that says that the outcome of our life is predetermined and nothing we can say or do will change it. Through the agency of Karma, each one of us creates our future circumstances by the actions we take today. When we understand this, we have great cause for hope and optimism. Therefore, we are advised to study deeply the law of Karma as it relates to our life:

He who unveils through study and meditation its intricate paths,
and throws light on those dark ways, in the windings of which so
many men perish owing to their ignorance of the labyrinth of life,
is working for the good of his fellow-men (2:305).

Metaphysical Mountaineers

Like the formidable presence of Mt. Everest, at once majestic and
mysterious, *The Secret Doctrine* towers above the terrain of esoteric
literature. Silently, but irresistibly, it beckons the adventuresome,
the dauntless—"those who called it forth," in the words of HPB—
to leave the arid steppes of mediocrity and materialism and scale
its mighty heights from where one may behold vast vistas of metaphysical splendor.

Those of lesser stamina (and driven largely by curiosity) often
make the attempt but soon give up, confused and dazed by the vertical labyrinth of esoteric lore; other gentle souls, unprepared for
the rigors of abstract metaphysical thought, find *The Secret Doctrine* to be a most effective soporific. But the sturdy mountaineer,
armed with the will to prevail, may profit from the advice of those
who have ascended the peaks.

"Remember that when one idea is well understood, it will help
in comprehending another, because the teachings are all interrelated," says Geoffrey Barborka.[41] Speaking of *The Secret Doctrine*,
Ernest Wood offers this perspective:

> It is not as psychic revelation that this mountain of philoso-
> phy plus science plus religion is presented. On the contrary, its
> author requests the reader to study the ideas and information
> given in it from the standpoint of common experience and rea-
> son. . . . She would advise one to accept nothing that is offensive
> to reason, or to our instincts and impulses of goodness and love,

or to the fundamental freedom and dignity of every man's own judgment.[42]

While a single ascent of Kilimanjaro, the Matterhorn, or Everest will at once reward the climber with a breathtaking and pristine view, the same cannot be said of Blavatsky's magnum opus. One must return again and again before the eyes become accustomed to the view at this altitude. "If anyone thinks that he knows *The Secret Doctrine* by reading it once or even a dozen times, or a score of times," advises G. de Purucker, "he mistakes greatly the situation. It must be read not only between the lines but within the words."[43]

But with repeated attempts comes familiarity with the terrain, increasing confidence, and the ability to find new footholds leading to still higher elevations. To his delight, the persevering climber finds that what was once considered to be *terra incognita* has become *terra firma*, while the lowlands from which the ascent began take on a crepuscular glow of unreality and illusion.

Appendix A

The Golden Stairs

A clean life, an open mind,
A pure heart, an eager intellect,
An unveiled spiritual perception,
A brotherliness for all,
A readiness to give and receive advice and instruction,
A loyal sense of duty to the Teacher,
A willing obedience to the behests of TRUTH,
Once we have placed our confidence in,
And believe that Teacher to be in possession of it;
A courageous endurance of personal injustice,
A brave declaration of principles,
A valiant defense of those who are unjustly attacked,
And a constant eye to the ideal of human progression,
And perfection which the secret science depicts—
These are the golden stairs
Up the steps of which the learner may climb
To the Temple of Divine Wisdom.

—H. P. Blavatsky

Appendix B

THE THEOSOPHICAL WORLDVIEW

The Theosophical Society, while reserving for each member full freedom to interpret those teachings known as Theosophy, is dedicated to preserving and realizing the Ageless Wisdom, which embodies both a worldview and a vision of human self-transformation. This tradition is founded upon certain fundamental propositions:

1. The universe and all that exists within it are one interrelated and interdependent whole.
2. Every existent being—from atom to galaxy—is rooted in the same universal, life-creating Reality. This Reality is all pervasive, but it can never be summed up in its parts, since it transcends all its expressions. It reveals itself in the purposeful, ordered, and meaningful processes of nature as well as in the deepest recesses of the mind and spirit.
3. Recognition of the unique value of every living being expresses itself in reverence for life, compassion for all, sympathy with the need of all individuals to find truth for themselves, and respect for all religious traditions. The ways in which these ideals become realities in individual life are both the privileged choice and the responsible act of every human being.

Central to the concerns of Theosophy is the desire to promote understanding and brotherhood among people of all races, nationalities, philosophies, and religions. Therefore, all people, whatever their race, creed, sex, caste, or color, are invited to participate equally in the life and work of the Society. The Theosophical Society imposes no dogmas but points toward the source of unity beyond all differences. Devotion to truth, love for all living beings, and commitment to a life of active altruism are the marks of the true Theosophist.

NOTES

Chapter 1

1. Anton Chekhov, "A Dreary Story," in *Anton Chekhov Short Stories,* trans. Constance Garnett (London: Folio Society, 2001), 87–138.

2. Aulus Persius Flaccus, *Satires,* 5:65.

3. Delivered on behalf of H. P. Blavatsky by Bertram Keightley to the Fourth Annual Convention of the Theosophical Society in America at the Palmer House, Chicago, Illinois, April 27, 1890.

4. Clara Codd, *Trust Yourself to Life* (Wheaton, IL: Theosophical Publishing House, 1975), 68–69.

Chapter 2

1. A. T. Barker, trans. and comp., Vicente Hao Chin, ed., *The Mahatma Letters to A. P. Sinnett in Chronological Sequence* (Adyar, Chennai: Theosophical Publishing House, 1998), no. 1, 3.

2. Lucius Annaeus Seneca, *Letters from a Stoic,* ed. Robin Campbell (London: Folio Society, 2003), no. 123, 188–89.

3. Thomas á Kempis, *Imitation of Christ,* ch. 1, "Imitating Christ and Despising All Vanities on Earth," in *Christian Classics Ethereal Library,* accessed December 5, 2018, http://www.ccel.org/ccel/kempis/imitation.ONE.1.html.

4. Timothy Keller, *The Reason for God: Belief in an Age of Skepticism* (London: Penguin Books, 2009), 58.

5. Aristotle, *Ethics,* 1103a15.

6. Johann Wolfgang von Goethe, in *The Complete Works of Johann Wolfgang von Goethe,* trans. Hjalman H. Boyesen (Colorado Springs: CreateSpace Publishing, 2015), 16.

7. Arthur C. Clarke, *Profiles of the Future* (New York: Harper & Row, 1962), ch. 2.

8. H. P. Blavatsky, *Collected Writings,* comp. Boris de Zirkoff (Wheaton, IL: Theosophical Publishing House, 1980), 1:130.

9. Seneca, *Letters,* no. 122, 186.

10. Saint Augustine, *Confessions,* trans. Albert C. Outler (Nashville: Thomas Nelson Publishers, 1999), 57.

11. Barker and Hao Chin, *Mahatma Letters,* no. 1, 3.

12. Ibid., no. 2, 6.

13. James Fenimore Cooper, *The American Democrat* (London: Forgotten Books, 2012), 183.

14. Paul Tillich, *The Shaking of the Foundations* (New York: Charles Scribner's Sons, 1948), 59, 63.

15. Cornelius Tacitus, *The Histories* (Oxford, England: Oxford University Press, 2008), bk. 4, ch. 6, 174.

16. Edmund Burke, "Speech on the Middlesex Election," February 7, 1771, in *Edmund Burke: Selected Writings and Speeches* (Washington, DC: Gateway Editions, 1997), 363.

17. George Orwell, *1984* (New York: Signet Classics, 1961), 321.

18. Thomas Hobbes, *Leviathan* (London: Folio Society, 2012), 72.

19. Mabel Collins, *Light on the Path* (Adyar, Chennai: Theosophical Publishing House, 1982), 26.

20. Houston Smith, *The World's Religions* (San Francisco: Harper San Francisco, 1991), 15.

21. John Ruskin, *Unto This Last* (Glasgow, Scotland: Grant Educational Co., 1920), essay 4, 116.

22. Clara Codd, *So Rich a Life* (Pretoria, South Africa: Institute for Theosophical Publications, 1951), 430.

23. Tacitus, *Histories*, bk. 4, ch. 6, 174.

24. Plutarch, *Lives,* 4:382–83.

25. Michel de Montaigne, *The Complete Essays* (London: Penguin Classics, 1993), 170.

26. L. W. Rogers, *Hints to Students of Occultism* (Chicago: Theo Book Company, 1931), 21.

Chapter 3

1. Francis Bacon, *Essays,* ed. Brian Vickers (London: Folio Society, 2002), 178–79.

2. Cicero, *Orations,* trans. D. H. Berry (London: Folio Society, 2011), 168.

3. Wilfred Thesiger, *Arabian Sands* (London: Penguin Classics, 2008), 329.

4. Thomas Sowell, "An Old Newness," *Jewish World Review,* April 29, 2008, http://jewishworldreview.com/cols/sowell042908.php3.

5. Alexis de Tocqueville, *Democracy in America*, trans. and ed. Harvey C. Mansfield and Delba Winthrop (Chicago: University of Chicago Press, 2000), 673.

6. Flannery O'Connor, "A Late Encounter with the Enemy," in *A Circle in the Fire and Other Stories* (London: Folio Society, 2013), 53.

7. Sri Madhava Ashish, *Man, Son of Man* (Wheaton, IL: Theosophical Publishing House, 1970), 38.

8. Seneca, *Letters,* no. 2, 3 (see ch. 2, n. 2).

9. Ralph Waldo Emerson, "Books," ch. 8 in *The Complete Works of Ralph Waldo Emerson, RWE.org*, last modified 2015, http://www.rwe.org/chapter-viii-books/.

10. Ibid.

11. I. K. Taimni, "Spiritual Life and Perception," *Theosophist* 93 (May 1972): 112.

12. H. P. Blavatsky, *The Key to Theosophy* (Wheaton, IL: Theosophical Publishing House, 1981), 32.

13. Annie Besant, *Thought Power: Its Control and Culture* (Wheaton, IL: Theosophical Publishing House, 1973), 33–34.

14. Bacon, *Essays*, 178.

Chapter 4

1. The word *happiness* corresponds to the Greek *eudaimonia*, but the modern connotations of *happiness* lack the richness of the Greek word. For Aristotle, happiness was not the same thing as pleasure. It was not a state or a feeling. In book one of the *Nicomachean Ethics* (1095a15), he defines it as an "activity of the soul in accordance with virtue."

2. Clara Codd, *The Way of the Disciple* (Adyar, Chennai: Theosophical Publishing House, 1988), 204.

3. Epictetus, "The Enchiridion," 11, trans. Elizabeth Carter, accessed October 2018, http://classics.mit.edu/Epictetus/epicench.html.

4. H. P Blavatsky published "The Golden Stairs" as a writing in a letter from a Master in 1890. Its thirteen phrases have been called the Ten Commandments of the Ancient Wisdom. See appendix A for the full text.

5. Maurice Possley, "Always Knew I Was Innocent," *Chicago Tribune*, November 24, 2006.

6. The moniker HPB is more than just a convenient acronym for the name Helena Petrovna Blavatsky. For further explanation, see the essay in chapter 10 of this book, entitled "HPB: A Perpetual Enigma."

7. Thomas Paine, "The American Crisis," pamphlet 1, December 19, 1776.

8. From the poem "The Winter Walk at Noon," which appeared in book 6 of William Cowper's *The Task* (1785).

9. N. Sri Ram, *Seeking Wisdom* (Adyar: Theosophical Publishing House, 1966), 4.

10. Paramahansa Yogananda, trans., *God Talks with Arjuna: The Bhagavad Gita* (Los Angeles: Self-Realization Fellowship, 1996), 1:296.

11. Cicero, in *Cicero on the Good Life*, trans. Michael Grant (London: Folio Society, 2003), 29.

12. Oliver Wendell Holmes, *The Poet at the Breakfast Table* (New York: Houghton, Mifflin and Company, 1900), 264.

13. Herbert A. Simon, "Designing Organizations for an Information-Rich World," in Martin Greenberger, *Computers, Communication, and the Public Interest* (Baltimore. MD: Johns Hopkins Press, 1971), 40–41.

14. Sir Edwin Arnold, *The Light of Asia* (New York: Dodd, Mead & Company, 1926), 177.

15. T. S. Eliot, *The Sacred Wood: Essays on Poetry and Criticism* (Mineola, NY: Dover Publications, 1997), 30.

16. T. S. Eliot, *Selected Prose of T. S. Eliot* (New York: Farrar, Straus and Giroux, 1975), 257.

Chapter 5

1. Ralph Waldo Emerson, *The Essential Writings of Ralph Waldo Emerson* (New York: Modern Library, 2000), 253.

2. Jiddu Krishnamurti, *At the Feet of the Master* (Wheaton, IL: Theosophical Publishing House, 1967), 9–10.

3. Mabel Collins, *Light on the Path*, 66 (see ch. 2, n. 19).

4. Aristotle, *Ethics,* 1156a5–1156b35.

5. Barker and Hao Chin, *Mahatma Letters,* no. 88, 274 (see ch. 2, n. 1).

6. David Shenk, quoted in Tom Regan, "Executives Learn to See through the 'Data Smog,'" *Christian Science Monitor,* August 1, 2007.

7. Annie Besant, trans., *The Bhagavad Gita* (Adyar, Chennai: Theosophical Publishing House, 1985), 188.

8. Annie Besant and Charles Leadbeater, *Talks on the Path of Occultism* (Adyar, Chennai: Theosophical Publishing House, 1980), 1:126.

9. Seneca, *Letters,* no. 2, 3 (see ch. 2, n. 2).

10. For the entire Theosophical Worldview statement, see appendix B.

11. Annie Besant, *The Universal Law of Life* (Adyar, Chennai: Theosophical Publishing House, 1992), 17.

12. I. K. Taimni, *The Science of Yoga* (Wheaton, IL: Theosophical Publishing House, 1961), 6.

13. Swami Madhavananda, trans., *Viveka-Cūdāmani* (Calcutta, India: Advaita Ashrama, 1989), 26.

14. Krishnamurti, *At the Feet of the Master,* 52.

15. Nicholas Carr, *The Shallows: What the Internet Is Doing to Our Brains* (New York: W. W. Norton & Company, 2010), 115–16.

16. Ibid., 132.

17. Collins, *Light on the Path*, 66.

18. Gordon Hempton, *One Square Inch of Silence: One Man's Search for Silence in a Noisy World* (New York: Atria Books, 2010), 1.

Chapter 6

1. Daniel Gross, "Children for Sale," *Slate,* May 24, 2006, http://www.slate.com/articles/business/moneybox/2006/05/children_for_sale.html.

2. Gudrun Schultz, "France Boosts Birth Rate with Incentives for Parents," *LifeSiteNews*, March 30, 2006, https://www.lifesitenews.com/news/france-boosts-birth-rate-with-incentives-for-parents.

3. Ian Stevenson interviewed thousands of children who were said to have past-life memories. Using rigorous scientific procedures to eliminate those cases that had more plausible explanations, he published his first ground-breaking book, *Twenty Cases Suggestive of Reincarnation* (Charlottesville, VA: University of Virginia Press, 1980), which detailed the cases of twenty children whose past-life memories he thought were authentic.

4. Lyrics from Frank Sinatra's signature song, "That's Life."

5. Sri Madhava Ashish, *Man, Son of Man*, 47–48 (see ch. 3, n. 7).

6. Cicero, "On Old Age," in *Cicero on the Good* Life, 188 (see ch. 4, n. 11). Cicero wrote this essay, along with some of his other most enduring works, while in exile at his country home in Tusculum a few years before he was assassinated for political reasons.

7. Alfred, Lord Tennyson, in *Tennyson's Poetry,* ed. Robert W. Hill, Jr (New York: W. W. Norton & Company, 1999), 82.

8. Virgil, in *Virgil: The Aeneid,* trans. C. Day Lewis (Oxford: Oxford University Press, 2009), 181.

9. Seneca, *Hercules Furens*, trans. Frank Justus Miller, *Theoi Classical Texts Library*, accessed January 14, 2019, https://www.theoi.com/Text/SenecaHerculesFurens.html.

10. N. Sri Ram, *The Human Interest* (Adyar: Theosophical Publishing House, 1950), 51.

Chapter 7

1. According to Mme. Blavatsky, the Stanzas of Dzyan are of Tibetan origin. They form the basis for her major work, *The Secret Doctrine.*

2. Literally, *pralaya* means "dissolution." It signifies a state of rest or inactivity between two life cycles (*manvantaras*) of the universe. Pralaya is the opposite of a manvantara.

3. H. P. Blavatsky, *Transactions of the Blavatsky Lodge* (Covina, CA: Theosophical University Press, 1946), 10.

4. The Theosophical Society in America has always had members who tried to help rehabilitate prisoners through books and literature. The earliest documentation of prison outreach I know of is a report by the Prison Work Bureau given at the Theosophical Society's Twenty-Seventh Annual Convention, held in Chicago on September 4–8, 1913.

5. S. Radhakrishnan, *Brihadaranyaka Upanishad*, in *The Principle Upanishads* (New Delhi: Harper Collins, 1995), ch. 4, sect. 3, vs. 2–6.

6. Gottfried de Purucker, *Occult Glossary* (Pasadena, CA: Theosophical University Press, 1996), 150.

7. According to HPB, an Initiate was "anyone who was received into and had revealed to him [or her] the mysteries and secrets of either Masonry or Occultism." See H. P. Blavatsky, *Theosophical Glossary* (Los Angeles: Theosophy Company, 1973), 156.

8. Blavatsky, *Collected Writings,* 12:599 (see ch. 2, n. 8).

9. I. K. Taimni, *Man, God and the Universe* (Wheaton, IL: Theosophical Publishing House, 1974), 367.

10. Barker and Hao Chin, *The Mahatma Letters*, no. 68, 200 (see ch. 2, n. 1).

Chapter 8

1. Shirley Nicholson, "Doctrine and Dogma," *American Theosophist* 71, no. 9 (October 1983): 296.

2. Josephine Ransom, *A Short History of the Theosophical Society* (Adyar, Chennai: Theosophical Publishing House, 1938), 5.

3. Robert Frost, "Robert Frost on Poet Amy Lowell," *The Christian Science Monitor,* May 16, 1925.

4. Henry Steel Olcott, *Old Diary Leaves: The History of the Theosophical Society*, 6 vols. (Adyar, Madras: Theosophical Publishing House, 1895–1935), 2:375.

5. Ibid.

6. Richard Ihle, "Jonathan Livingston Theosopher," *American Theosophist* 75, no. 10 (November 1987): 351.

7. Nicholson, "Doctrine and Dogma," 296.

8. Joy Mills, "Theosophical Education: On the Difference between Dogma and Doctrine," *American Theosophist* 75, no. 6 (June 1987): 212.

9. Emily Sellon, "Some Reflections on a Theosophical World-View," *American Theosophist* 71, no. 7 (July 1983): 244.

10. From G. de Purucker's editorial entitled "The Real Work of the T. S." published in the journal *The Theosophical Forum*, sometime between the years of 1937–1942. It later appeared in Purucker's book *Messages to Conventions and Other Writings* (Covina, CA: Theosophical University Press, 1943).

11. Montaigne, *Complete Essays*, 170 (see ch. 2, n. 25).

12. Cicero, "On Old Age," in *Cicero on the Good* Life, 188 (see ch. 4, n. 11).

13. T. S. Eliot, *Selected Prose*, 102 (see ch. 4, n. 16).

14. Letter from H. P. Blavatsky to the Second American Convention of the Theosophical Society, held in Chicago on April 22 and 23, 1888.

15. Lionel Trilling, "Manners, Morals, and the Novel," in *The Moral Obligation to Be Intelligent* (Chicago: Northwestern University Press, 2009), 118.

16. Originally written in French under the title "Legende sur la Belle de Nuit," the English translation appears in Blavatsky, *Collected Writings*, 1:7–9 (see ch. 2, n. 8).

17. Barker and Hao Chin, *Mahatma Letters,* no. 2, 9 (see ch. 2, n. 1).

18. This moniker comes from the Blavatsky Lecture entitled "H. P. Blavatsky, the Light-Bringer," which Geoffrey Barborka delivered to the London Theosophical Society in 1970.

Chapter 9

1. Ernest Wood, *Taking Charge of Your Life* (Wheaton, IL: Theosophical Publishing House, 1985), 113.

2. Blavatsky, *Key to Theosophy,* 138 (see ch. 3, n. 12).

3. Johann Wolfgang von Goethe, *Faust: A Tragedy,* ed. Cyrus Hamlin, trans. Walter Arndt (New York: W. W. Norton & Company, 1998), 12.

4. Adelaide Gardner, *Introductory Studies in Theosophy* (London: Theosophical Publishing House, 1964), 49.

5. For a complete history of the Society's three Objects, see chapter 3 of John Algeo's *Unlocking the Door: Studies in the Key to Theosophy* (Wheaton: Theosophical Publishing House, 2001).

6. Rohit Mehta, "The Three Objects," *American Theosophist* 41, no. 13 (March 1953): 56.

7. Radha Burnier, *Human Regeneration* (Amsterdam: Uitgeverij der Theosofische Vereniging, 1990), 25.

8. Joy Mills, "The Third Object of the Theosophical Society," *American Theosophist* 58, no. 10 (October 1970): 297.

9. Hugh Shearman, "Ourselves and Nature," *Theosophist* 64 (February 1943): 373.

10. Krishnamurti, *At the Feet of the Master,* 31–32 (see ch. 5, n. 2).

11. Joy Mills, *American Theosophist* 58, no. 10 (October 1970): 297.

12. Henry S. Olcott's inaugural address was delivered at Mott Memorial Hall, New York City, November 18, 1875. See *Inaugural Address of Four Presidents of the Theosophical Society: H. S. Olcott, Annie Besant, George S. Arundale, C. Jinarajadasa* (Adyar, Chennai: Theosophical Publishing House, 1946), 21.

13. Barker and Hao Chin, *Mahatma Letters,* no. 92, 299 (see ch. 2, n. 1).

Chapter 10

1. John Algeo, *Getting Acquainted with* The Secret Doctrine (Wheaton: Theosophical Society in America, 2007), 3.

2. R. H., "Review: *The Voice of the Silence,*" *Theosophist* 11 (February 1890): 281.

3. Annie Besant, quoted by Boris de Zirkoff in his introduction to *The Voice of the Silence* (Wheaton, IL, Quest Books, 1992), 24a–25a.

4. Olcott, *Old Diary Leaves:* 1:208–9 (see ch. 8, n. 4).

5. G. R. S. Mead, from a letter originally published in *Lucifer,* vol. 8, June 1891, 295–6, and quoted by Boris de Zirkoff in his introduction to the 1992 edition of Blavatsky's *The Voice of the Silence,* 35a–36a.

6. H. P. Blavatsky, *The Voice of the Silence*, centenary edition (Adyar, Chennai: Theosophical Publishing House, 1982), 6.

7. Ibid.

8. Bhikshu Sangharakshita, *Paradox and Poetry in* The Voice of the Silence (Bangalore, India: Indian Institute of World Culture, 1958), 10–11.

9. Although Rohit Mehta's *The Creative Silence* is out of print, a digital copy is available at www.Theosophical.org/online-resources/books.

10. William Kingsland, *The Real H. P. Blavatsky: A Study in Theosophy, and a Memoir of a Great Soul* (London: John M. Watkins, 1928), vii.

11. Gottfried de Purucker, *H. P. Blavatsky: The Mystery* (San Diego: Point Loma Publications, 1974), 1.

12. Herbert Burrows, quoted by Boris de Zirkoff in his introduction to the 1992 edition of Blavatsky's *The Voice of the Silence*, 20a–21a.

13. Gordon L. Plummer, "H. P. Blavatsky: The Mystery," *American Theosophist* 57, no. 5 (May 1969): 145.

14. H. P. Blavatsky, *The Voice of the Silence* (Adyar, India: Theosophical Publishing House, 1944), 101.

15. Kingsland, *The Real H. P. Blavatsky*, 119, fn.

16. Besant, *Bhagavad Gita*, 67 (see ch. 5, n. 7).

17. Lao Tsu, *Tao Te Ching: The Classic Book of Integrity and the Way*, trans. Victor H. Mair (New York: Bantam Books, 1990), 15.

18. Seneca, *Letters from a Stoic*, 3 (see ch. 2, n. 2).

19. Beatrice Bruteau, "The Validity of Mysticism," *Theosophist* 111 (May 1990): 299.

20. Evelyn Underhill, *Mystics of the Church* (Harrisburg, PA: Morehouse Publishing, 1975), 9.

21. Evelyn Underhill, *Practical Mysticism* (Columbus, OH: Ariel Press, 1942), 23.

22. Bruteau, "The Validity of Mysticism," 300.

Chapter 11

1. (Attributed to) H. P. Blavatsky, *Lucifer* 9, no. 49 (September 1891): 4.

2. Ibid.

3. Joy Mills, *From Inner to Outer Transformation* (Amsterdam: Uitgeverij der Theosofische Vereniging, 1996), 37.

4. Eknath Easwaran, trans., *The Upanishads* (Tomales, CA: Nilgiri Press, 1996), 109.

5. J. Krishnamurti, *The First and Last Freedom* (San Francisco: Harper San Francisco, 1975), 249.

6. Lao Tsu, *Tao Te Ching*, trans. Stephen Mitchell (New York: HarperCollins, 1988), 1.

7. Thomas Merton, *New Seeds of Contemplation* (New York: New Directions Books, 1961), 228.

8. Mu Soeng, trans., *The Diamond Sutra: Transforming the Way We Perceive the World* (Boston, MA: Wisdom Publications, 2000), 89.

9. Eknath Easwaran, trans., *The Dhammapada* (Tomales, CA: 1985), 125.

10. John Ruskin, *Modern Painters* (New York: Alfred A. Knopf, 1988), 250.

11. Blavatsky, *Key to Theosophy*, 37 (see ch. 3, n. 12).

12. Ibid., 130.

13. John Stuart Mill, "On Nature" (1874); repr. in *Three Essays on Religion: Nature, the Utility of Religion, and Theism* (Spartanburg, SC: Reprint Publishers, 2016), 14.

14. Ibid.

15. Blavatsky, *Key to Theosophy*, 121.

16. Francis Bacon, *Novum Organum* (1620), trans. James Spedding, bk. 1, aphorism 129; *Wikisource*, accessed November 9, 2018, https://en.wikisource. org/wiki/Novum_Organum/Book_I_(Spedding).

17. Mill, "On Nature," 14.

18. Alexander Pope, "An Essay on Criticism," originally published in 1711; repr. in *Poetry Foundation*, last modified October 13, 2009, accessed November 8, 2018, https://www.poetryfoundation.org/articles/69379/an-essay-on-criticism.

19. Mill, "On Nature," 25.

20. Blavatsky, *Key to Theosophy,* 37.

21. Ivan Turgenev, *Fathers and Sons* (London: Penguin Classics, 1965), 116.

22. N. Sri Ram, *The Way of Wisdom* (Adyar: Theosophical Publishing House, 1993), 223.

23. Flower Newhouse, *Angels of Nature* (Wheaton, IL: Quest Books, 1995), 128.

24. Barker and Hao Chin, *Mahatma Letters,* no. 47, 129 (see ch. 2, n. 1).

25. Stephen Mitchell, trans., *Bhagavad Gita: A New Translation* (New York: Harmony Books, 2002), 65.

26. Joseph Hall, *Bishop Hall's Works,* vol. 7 (Oxford: D. A. Talboys, 1837), 153.

27. Flavius Arrianus Xenophon, *The Campaigns of Alexander* (London: Folio Society, 2012), 132.

28. St. Teresa of Ávila, in *Goodreads*, accessed January 7, 2019, https://www. goodreads.com/quotes/260639.

29. Kathleen Norris, *Dakota: A Spiritual Geography* (New York: Ticknor & Fields, 1993), 15.

30. Radhakrishnan, *Brihadaranyaka Upanishad*, ch. 1, sect. 3, vs. 28 (see ch. 7, n. 5).

31. C. W. Leadbeater, *The Inner Life* (Wheaton, IL: Theosophical Publishing House, 1978), 131.

32. Fyodor Dostoevsky, quoted in Viktor E. Frankl, *Man's Search for Meaning* (Boston, MA, 2006), 86.

33. Somerset Maugham's original statement was most likely, "Only a mediocre writer is always at his best"; see *Goodreads*, accessed January 7, 2019, https://www.goodreads.com/quotes/52581.

34. Annie Besant, *The Spiritual Life* (Wheaton: Theosophical Publishing House, 1991), 18.

35. Codd, *Way of the Disciple,* 204 (see ch. 4, n. 2).

36. Thucydides, quoted in Robert Burton, *The Anatomy of Melancholy* (1621; repr. London: Folio Society, 2010), 1:23.

37. Lao Tsu, *Tao Te Ching*, trans. Gia-Fu Feng and Jane English (New York: Vintage Books, 1989), 58.

38. John Henry Newman, *The Idea of University* (Colorado Springs: CreateSpace Publishing, 2016), 177.

39. C. S. Lewis, *Mere Christianity* (London: Macmillan, 1952), 125.

40. Gottfried de Purucker, *Fundamentals of the Esoteric Philosophy* (Covina, CA: Theosophical University Press, 1947), 385–86.

41. Aldous Huxley, *Perennial Philosophy* (New York: Harper & Row, 1970), vii.

42. Sri Madhava Ashish, "The Value of Uncertainty," *American Theosophist* 67, no. 1 (January 1979): 10.

43. *Nidana* is a Sanskrit word, the meanings of which include "chain of causation" or "primary or first cause." It is found in the Rig Veda and other Hindu scriptures.

44. St. Cyprian, "Epistle 1 to Donatus," *New Advent*, accessed November 8, 2018, http://www.newadvent.org/fathers/050601.htm.

45. Barker and Hao Chin, *Mahatma Letters,* no. 15, 49.

46. John Milton, *Paradise Lost* (1667; repr. London: Folio Society, 2003), 82.

47. Blavatsky, *Key to Theosophy*, 121–122.

48. Ibid., 121.

49. Barker and Hao Chin, *Mahatma Letters,* no. 92, 294.

50. Bacon, *Essays,* 140 (see ch. 3, n. 1).

51. Attributed to H. P. Blavatsky, "There Is a Road," *Lucifer* 9 (September 1891): 4.

52. Blavatsky, *Key to Theosophy,* 145.

53. Barker and Hao Chin, *Mahatma Letters,* no. 2, 8.

54. Blavatsky, *Key to Theosophy,* 135.

55. Ibid.

56. Confucius, *The Analects* (London: Penguin Classics, 1979), 107.

57. C. Jinarajadasa, "The Discovery of Truth through Service," *Theosophist* 71 (February 1950): 345.

58. Annie Besant, *From the Outer Court to the Inner Sanctum* (Wheaton: Theosophical Publishing House, 1983), 1–2.

59. Ibid., 4.

60. Mircea Eliade, *The Myth of the Eternal Return* (Princeton, NJ: Princeton University Press, 2005), 18.

61. Milton, *Paradise Lost*, 35.

62. Geoffrey Hodson, *Call to the Heights* (Wheaton, IL: Theosophical Publishing House, 1987), 118.

63. Geoffrey Hodson, *The Yogic Ascent to the Spiritual Heights* (Manila, Philippines: Stellar Books, 1991), 214.

64. Barker and Hao Chin, *Mahatma Letters,* no. 54, 148.

Chapter 12

1. Sellon, "Some Reflections," 244 (see ch. 8, n. 9).

2. William Congreve, *Love for Love* (1695), act 5, sc. 3; see *Project Gutenberg*, accessed January 14, 2019, http://www.gutenberg.org/files/1244/1244-h/1244-h.htm.

3. *The Secret Doctrine* in italics refers to the book, but when listed without italics, the term refers to a body of teachings.

4. Barker and Hao Chin, *Mahatma Letters*, no. 1, 4 (see ch. 2, n. 1).

5. Lord Byron, *Don Juan*, Canto 15, stanza 99, lines 3–4.

6. William Wordsworth, "Sonnets from River Duddon: After-Thought," line 14.

7. Emerson, *Essential Writings*, 238 (see ch. 5, n. 1).

8. Plutarch, *Lives*, ed. Arthur Hugh Clough, trans. John Dryden (London: Folio Society, 2010), 1:202.

9. Ibid., 1:203.

10. Emerson, *Essential Writings*, 237.

11. Beethoven, quoted in David Tame, *The Secret Power of Music* (Rochester: Destiny Books, 1984), 19.

12. Barker and Hao Chin, *Mahatma Letters*, no.1, 4.

13. John Locke, "Dedicatory Epistle," in *An Essay Concerning Humane Understanding*, vol. 1 (1690). See Project Gutenberg, accessed January 8, 2019, http://www.gutenberg.org/files/10615/10615-h/10615-h.htm.

14. Edmund Burke, from the political pamphlet *Reflections on the Revolution in France* (1790). See Project Gutenberg, accessed January 8, 2019, http://www.gutenberg.org/files/15679/15679-h/15679-h.htm#REFLECTIONS.

15. St. Augustine, *Confessions,* book 11, 264 (see ch. 2, n. 10).

16. Ibid., 266.

17. Marcus Aurelius, *Meditations* (New York: Alfred A. Knopf, 1992), 40.

18. Marguerite Yourcenar, *Memoirs of Hadrian,* trans. Grace Frick (New York: Farrar, Straus and Giroux, 2005), 26.

19. Yogi Ramacharaka, comp., *The Spirit of the Upanishads* (Chicago: Yogi Publication Society, 1907), 9.

20. S. Radhakrishnan, ed. and trans., *The Principal Upanishads* (New Dehli: Harper Collins, 1953), 582.

21. Ramacharaka, *Spirit of the Upanishads,* 11.

22. Purucker, *Fundamentals,* 2 (see ch. 11, n. 40).

23. Taimni, *Man, God and the Universe,* 1–2 (see ch. 7, n. 9).

24. Easwaran, *Upanishads,* 125 (see ch. 11, n. 4).

25. Blavatsky, *Key to Theosophy,* 51 (see ch. 3, n. 12).

26. Blavatsky, *Theosophical Glossary,* 113 (see ch. 7, n. 7).

27. Blavatsky, *Key to Theosophy,* 36, fn.

28. Blavatsky, *Transactions,* 33 (see ch. 7, n. 3).

29. Geoffrey Barborka, *Secret Doctrine Questions & Answers* (San Diego: Wizards Bookshelf, 2003), 24.

30. Ibid., 92.

31. Purucker, *Occult Glossary,* 91 (see ch. 7, n. 6).

32. Geoffrey Barborka, *The Divine Plan* (Adyar, Chennai: Theosophical Publishing House, 1961), 57.

33. Annie Besant, *The Ancient Wisdom* (Adyar: Theosophical Publishing House, 1986), 225.

34. Gottfried de Purucker, *Dialogues of G. de Purucker,* ed. Arthur L. Conger, 3 vols. (Covina, CA: Theosophical University Press, 1948), 2:400–401.

35. Barborka, *Divine Plan,* 420.

36. Blavatsky, *Theosophical Glossary,* 187.

37. Judith Tyberg (1902–1980) was author of the groundbreaking work *Sanskrit Keys to the Wisdom Religion* (1940; repr. San Diego, CA: Point Loma Publications, 1976), 98.

38. Gottfried de Purucker, *The Esoteric Tradition* (Pasadena, CA: Theosophical University Press, 1973), 1:456.

39. Tyberg, *Sanskrit Keys,* 27–28.

40. Cf. Acts 10:34: "God is no respecter of persons."

41. Barborka, *Divine Plan,* xiv.

42. Ernest Wood, *Secret Doctrine Digest* (Adyar, Chennai: Theosophical Publishing House, 1956), v–vi.

43. Purucker, *Fundamentals,* 202.

SELECTED BIBLIOGRAPHY

Listed below are the books to which I have referred in the writing of these essays. This selected bibliography does not include every title mentioned, nor does it necessarily represent all the sources I have consulted. However, it does indicate those works that I consider to have been influential in shaping and informing my views over a period of many years. Many of these books should be of interest to students of Theosophy, and the few non-Theosophical titles listed may be of interest to the general reader.

Aristotle. *Ethics.* Translated by J. A. K. Thomson. London: Folio Society, 2003.

Ashish, Sri Madhava. *Man, Son of Man.* Wheaton, IL: Theosophical Publishing House, 1970.

Augustine, Saint. *Confessions.* Translated by Albert C. Outler. Nashville: Thomas Nelson Publishers, 1999.

Bacon, Francis. *Francis Bacon Essays.* Edited by Brian Vickers. London: Folio Society, 2002.

Barborka, Geoffrey. *The Divine Plan.* Adyar, Chennai: Theosophical Publishing House, 1961.

_____. *Glossary of Sanskrit Terms.* San Diego: Point Loma Publications, 1973.

_____. *Secret Doctrine Questions & Answers.* San Diego: Wizards Bookshelf, 2003.

Barker, A. T., transcriber, Vicente Hao Chin, ed. *The Mahatma Letters to A. P. Sinnett in Chronological Sequence.* Adyar, Chennai: Theosophical Publishing House. 1998.

Besant, Annie. *Thought Power: Its Control and Culture.* Wheaton, IL: Theosophical Publishing House, 1973.

Besant, Annie, and Charles Leadbeater. *Talks on the Path of Occultism,* Vol. 1. Adyar, Chennai: Theosophical Publishing House, 1980.

Blavatsky, Helena Petrovna. *Isis Unveiled: Secrets of the Ancient Wisdom Tradition, Madame Blavatsky's First Work.* Abridgment by Michael Gomes. Wheaton, IL: Theosophical Publishing House, 1997.

————. *The Key to Theosophy.* Wheaton, IL: Theosophical Publishing House, 1981.

————. *The Secret Doctrine.* 3 vols. Adyar, Chennai: Theosophical Publishing House, 1979.

————. *Theosophical Glossary.* Los Angeles: Theosophy Company, 1973.

————. *Transactions of the Blavatsky Lodge.* Covina, CA: Theosophical University Press, 1946.

————. *The Voice of the Silence.* With notes and introduction by Arya Asanga. Adyar, Chennai: Theosophical Publishing House, 1944.

————. *The Voice of the Silence.* Centenary Edition. Adyar, Chennai: Theosophical Publishing House, 1982.

————. *The Voice of the Silence.* With an introduction by Boris de Zirkoff. Wheaton, IL: Theosophical Publishing House, 1992.

Burnier, Radha. *Human Regeneration.* Amsterdam: Uitgeverij der Theosofische Vereniging in Nederland, 1990.

Cicero, Marcus Tullius. *Cicero on the Good Life.* Translated by Michael Grant. London: Folio Society, 2003.

Codd, Clara. *Trust Yourself to Life.* Wheaton, IL: Theosophical Publishing House, 1975.

————. *The Way of the Disciple.* Adyar, Chennai: Theosophical Publishing House, 1988.

Collins, Mabel. *Light on the Path.* Adyar, Chennai: Theosophical Publishing House, 1982.

Gardner, Adelaide. *Introductory Studies in Theosophy.* London: Theosophical Publishing House, 1964.

Gomes, Michael. *The Dawning of the Theosophical Movement.* Wheaton, IL: Theosophical Publishing House, 1987.

Huxley, Aldous. *The Perennial Philosophy.* New York: Harper & Row, 1970.

Krishnamurti, Jiddu (Alcyone). *At the Feet of the Master.* Wheaton, IL: Theosophical Publishing House, 1967.

Leadbeater, Charles. *The Inner Life*: Wheaton, IL: Theosophical Publishing House, 1978.

_____. *Masters and the Path.* Adyar, Chennai: Theosophical Publishing House, 1992.

_____. *Talks on the Path of Occultism.* Vol. 2. Adyar, Chennai: Theosophical Publishing House, 1965.

Mehta, Rohit. *The Creative Silence.* Adyar, Chennai: Theosophical Publishing House, 1957.

Mills, Joy. *From Inner to Outer Transformation.* Amsterdam: Uitgeverij der Theosofische Vereniging in Nederland, 1996.

Montaigne, Michel de. *The Complete Essays of Montaigne.* Translated by Donald M. Frame. Stanford, CA: Stanford University Press, 2000.

Murphet, Howard. *When Daylight Comes.* Wheaton, IL: Theosophical Publishing House, 1975.

Nicholson, Shirley. *Ancient Wisdom, Modern Insight.* Wheaton, IL: Theosophical Publishing House, 1985.

Olcott, Henry Steel. *Old Diary Leaves: The History of the Theosophical Society.* 6 vols. Adyar, Madras: Theosophical Publishing House, 1895–1935.

Powell, A. E. *The Astral Body.* London: Theosophical Publishing House, 1965.

Purucker, Gottfried de. *Dialogues of G. de Purucker.* 3 vols. Covina, CA: Theosophical University Press, 1948.

_____. *Fundamentals of the Esoteric Philosophy.* Covina, CA: Theosophical University Press, 1947.

_____. *Messages to Conventions and Other Writings.* Covina, CA: Theosophical University Press, 1943.

_____. *Occult Glossary.* Pasadena, CA: Theosophical University Press, 1996.

Purucker, Gottfried de, and Katherine Tingley. *H. P. Blavatsky: The Mystery.* San Diego: Point Loma Publications, 1974.

Ransom, Josephine. *A Short History of the Theosophical Society.* Adyar, Chennai: Theosophical Publishing House, 1938.

Rogers, L. W. *Hints to Young Students of Occultism.* Chicago: Theo Book Company, 1931.

Seneca, Lucius Annaeus. *Letters from a Stoic.* Edited by Robin Campbell. London: Folio Society, 2003.

Smith, Huston. *The World's Religions.* San Francisco: HarperCollins, 1991.

Sri Ram, N. *Thoughts for Aspirants, Second Series.* Adyar, Chennai: Theosophical Publishing House, 1973.

Taimni, I. K. *Man, God and the Universe.* Wheaton, IL: Theosophical Publishing House, 1974.

Wood, Ernest. *Secret Doctrine Digest.* Adyar, Chennai: Theosophical Publishing House, 1956.

INDEX

Quest Books

encourages open-minded inquiry into
world religions, philosophy, science, and the arts
in order to understand the wisdom of the ages,
respect the unity of all life, and help people explore
individual spiritual self-transformation.

Its publications are generously supported by
The Kern Foundation,
a trust committed to Theosophical education.

Quest Books is the imprint of
The Theosophical Publishing House,
a division of the Theosophical Society in America.
For information about programs, literature,
on-line study, membership benefits, and international centers,
see www.theosophical.org
or call 800-669-1571 or (outside the U.S.) 630-668-1571.

Related Quest Titles

Ancient Wisdom, Modern Insight, by Shirley Nicholson

The Key to Theosophy, An Abridgment, by Joy Mills

The One True Adventure: Theosophy and the Quest for Meaning,
by Joy Mills

The Pilgrim Self: Traveling the Path from Life to Life,
by Robert Ellwood

The Secret Gateway: Modern Theosophy and the Ancient Wisdom Tradition,
by Edward Abdill

To order books or a complete Quest catalog,
Call 800-669-9425 or (outside the U.S.) 630-665-0130.